The Uncut Mystery—
It's So Much More
Than Hair

# Covered
## by Love

The Uncut Mystery—
It's So Much More
Than Hair

by Lori Wagner
and Gwyn Oakes

# Covered
## by Love

# Covered by Love
## The Uncut Mystery—It's So Much More Than Hair

by Lori Wagner and Gwyn Oakes

Cover and Interior Design: Laura Jurek

Printed in United States of America

A *More to Life* Publication
8855 Dunn Road
Hazelwood, MO 63042

THROUGH GOD'S WORD

# Table of Contents

# Acknowledgments

## Contributors

Marvin and Claudette Walker
Randy Cluster
Shirley Kennedy
Mary Loudermilk
Abigail Zuloga
Gabriella Thompson
Aleatha Morgan

Which aspect of your appearance do you fuss over the most? Talk about the most? For the majority of us, it's hair. There's just no getting around the fact: hair is important. Hair is important to God, too.

Girls of all ages, all over the world, belong to churches where biblical concepts of natural hair length are taught and lived out. If you are in this category, I want you to know you are on the right track, even if you've never understood all the reasons why.

> "A man can eat his dinner without understanding
> exactly how food nourishes him."
> —C. S. Lewis

In addition to cheering you on and providing clear information to help you define why you do what you do, this book has also been written for people new to these biblical concepts and those who have always wondered about "the hair thing."

Whatever category you are in right now, I hope as you read you will find answers that sit well in your spirit. And may all of us begin with open, prayerful attitudes to receive instruction from the Lord who leads us into all truth.

# Introductory Story

"Whatcha reading, Jackie?"

"A mystery."

Katelyn pushed her sunglasses back on her head and looked curiously at the girl sprawled across the plush down comforter. "I didn't know you liked mysteries."

"It's all your doing, Katie. I'm hooked on mysteries."

"My doing?"

"Yeah." Jackie marked her place, clapped the book shut, and sat on the edge of her bed. "Remember last year—that talk we had about modesty?"

"I don't think I'll ever forget that." A big grin spread across Katelyn's freckled face as she plopped down next to her friend. "You sure had me worried. But—wow—you don't seem to be struggling with things like you did back then."

"I'm not," Jackie said. "*The Girl in the Dress* helped me understand the importance of dressing modestly. Understanding 'why' makes it so much easier, and I'm really glad I'm not confused anymore."

"Me, too." Katelyn looked at the book Jackie held but could not make out the title hidden by Jackie's fingers. "OK. So what does that have to do with what you're reading now?"

"Well," Jackie drawled out the word into two long syllables then tucked the book inside her hoodie. "You want to know, huh?"

"What do you think?" Katelyn propped her hands on her hips and glared at the girl on the bed. *She looks way too much like my dog after he pulled the pizza box off the kitchen table.*

"Oh … you …" Quick as lightning, Katelyn grabbed Jackie's hood, pulled it over her head, and snatched the book from her hand.

"Hey! That's no way to treat your best friend!" Jackie sputtered.

"So, what's this about anyway?" Katelyn asked. "It doesn't look like a mystery to me."

"Well, you have to back up a minute. Do you remember the subtitle to *The Girl in the Dress*?"

"I sure do. Mom left it on the coffee table for three months to make sure I read it."

Jackie laughed out loud. "I didn't think you had any problems with modesty."

"I don't, really. Mom just wanted to make sure I understood so I can explain when people ask me why I dress the way I do."

"Good idea." Jackie folded her arms across her chest in her best school teacher pose. "So, Miss Katelyn Elizabeth, what was the subtitle?"

"*Uncovering the Mystery of Modesty*, Ms. Jaqueline."

"Right. See? *The Girl in the Dress* was about a mystery—the mystery of modesty. This one's about a mystery, too."

"*Covered by Love.* Is it another book about clothes?"

"It's a book about another mystery in the Bible—a different kind of covering—our hair."

"Hmm, the Bible does seem to have a lot of mysteries. I wonder why."

"I don't know all the answers, but I know God used that first Pure Path book to help me understand the mystery of modesty, and this one is helping me understand why we've been taught to not cut our hair."

"I guess that is kind of a mystery."

"Yeah," Jackie said. "And it's hard for new Christians to understand, too. I want to know the reasons why—for myself and so I can help others who might not understand. I don't get it all, but I've been in church long enough to know there's something special about this 'covering of love.'"

Katelyn leafed through a few pages. "Oh—there's some cool stuff in here. Styling tips. Treatments for split ends."

"Really?" Jackie said, "I didn't get that far."

"We went through the first book together," Katelyn said. "I'll give you your book back if you'll start at the beginning again—with me."

"You win."

She dropped the book into Jackie's hand and wrapped her arm around her friend's shoulder. The girls smiled at each other through their reflections in the mirror—two girls in dresses, two heads with long tresses.

13

"You know," Jackie said, "I've been looking in this mirror a lot lately, and I've been seeing things differently than I used to."

"How's that?"

"I keep remembering that Bible verse that says something like 'now we see through a glass darkly' and 'now we know in part.'"

"I know which one you mean," Katelyn said. "Someday we'll see and understand clearly. But that's in Heaven."

"Right," Jackie agreed. "But for now, I want to learn what I need to live in this world the way God wants me to. And—there's another Scripture verse that says something about the Bible and a mirror, how if we listen to the Word and don't do it, it's like looking in a mirror and forgetting what we look like. It's about being a doer, not just a hearer."

"Hey, girls." Jackie's mom peeked in the open door. "I love hearing you two talk like this, and I just wanted to make sure you know the last part of that verse."

"What is it, Mom?"

"It says that when we do what we know to do, we are blessed."

"I guess it's worth searching out a mystery if there's a blessing attached to it," said Katelyn.

"I'm up for some blessings," said Jackie. "Let's start right now."

## Chapter One

# Want to Know a Secret?

As you study,
please take time to
look up and read the verses
of Scripture that are noted
throughout this book.

# Want to Know a Secret?

Secrets are like salt on a pretzel: They add a little zip to the bread and make us thirsty. There's something about a **mystery** that attracts our attention and stirs up our curiosity to discover what's behind the hidden.

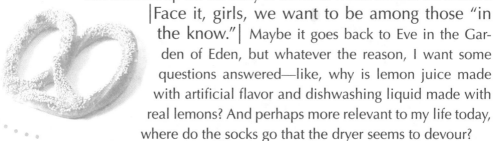

|Face it, girls, we want to be among those "in the know."| Maybe it goes back to Eve in the Garden of Eden, but whatever the reason, I want some questions answered—like, why is lemon juice made with artificial flavor and dishwashing liquid made with real lemons? And perhaps more relevant to my life today, where do the socks go that the dryer seems to devour?

There's something in most females that wants to "unlock our Sherlock" and be the one to tell the world important things, like, "It was Colonel Mustard in the library with the candlestick." I can't speak for everyone, but I have this inclination to be an unpuzzler—a code-cracking, riddle-revealing woman of the Word! Yes, I've been researching and praying and writing. This book, I believe with all my heart, has some answers for you about something that affects us all—our hair.

Those lovely strands on your scalp are there for a reason, and hair touches so much more than the tops of our heads. Hair is a symbol of much more than you might ever have imagined, and I believe you will have a new appreciation for your own cranial crown by the time you finish this book.

# Bible Mysteries

You've probably figured out by now there are mysteries in the Bible. A mystery is something that is or has been hidden, like a buried treasure—and God's Word is a vault of unending delights to discover. Although a mystery may not be known to the general masses, it is not necessarily hidden from everyone. It just hasn't been explained or known yet on a wide scale, and I'm so excited about sharing some beautiful treasures you may not have seen or known before. I hope you'll find yourself saying, "Oh! I get it! Isn't that beautiful? God is so good!"

# First Things First

When we're studying, reading, or listening to teaching, we first need to recognize the importance of showing proper respect to God and His Word. It is the beginning of wisdom (Proverbs 9:10). Without a "beginning" to our "getting" spiritual understanding, we'll have nothing more than a black hole where we could have had a well of wisdom. A black hole is not going to help us, but a well of wisdom to draw from would be awesome.

It's possible to have a lot of knowledge without having wisdom, and in this world, we can use healthy doses of both. Knowledge means we get

"Rabbit's clever," said Pooh thoughtfully.

"Yes," said Piglet, "Rabbit's clever."

"And he has Brain."

"Yes," said Piglet, "Rabbit has Brain."

There was a long silence.

"I suppose," said Pooh, "that that's why he never understands anything."[1]

facts and principles in our heads, but wisdom goes beyond just mentally understanding something.

The dictionary defines *wisdom* as "knowledge of what is true or right coupled with just judgment as to action."[2] Wisdom connects knowledge with discernment, which means to recognize or understand. It also has to do with having insight, or seeing the true nature of things. **[Wisdom = Knowledge + Understanding]** Our level of wisdom is displayed by the life choices we make.

Isaiah said, "For precept must be upon precept, precept upon precept; line upon line, line upon line; here a little, and there a little" (28:10).

"First things first" wouldn't be a popular saying if things didn't build one on top of another—if life had no priorities or order.

18

# God Is Not Haphazard – He Is a God of Order

God isn't haphazard in anything He does. He's a God of order and a master architect. The Bible says He placed the sun and moon right where He wanted them (Genesis 1:17). Creation was not a random fling of His holy hand to see where the sun, moon, and stars landed in space like darts on a dart board.

The orderliness of God's creation influenced people who changed their worlds. Scientific genius Sir Isaac Newton is famous for his studies on the laws of motion and gravity. What you might not know is that he spent more time studying the things of God than he spent studying and writing about science.[3]

Over his lifetime, Newton wrote approximately 1.3 million words on biblical subjects. He recognized that scientific methods followed orderly patterns established by God. He once wrote, "Gravity explains the motions of the planets, but it cannot explain who set the planets in motion. God governs all things."

The concepts he used worked in harmony with God's established, designed order. **It's exciting to think of the things we might discover when we work within God's established order.**

19

Part of God's order involves separation. *Separation* is a word that doesn't always give us warm, fuzzy feelings. By itself, it can bring to mind images of broken families, segregation, divisions, and the like. When it comes to God, separation is a good thing, and in the long run leads to acceptance, inclusion, and togetherness.

**God has always had a "doctrine of separation."** It's a principle that's been in His heart before He made the world. The very first day of creation He divided light from darkness. Separation means there is a contrast or notable difference. If there were no differences, there could be no separation.

God has boundaries, and destroying God's dividing lines is one of Satan's chief activities. He whispers in our ears, blurs God's Word, and attempts to alter what God created to be beautifully and wonderfully different. In the Garden of Eden, Satan stirred up questions that messed up Adam and Eve. They ended up stripped of their innocence and left naked and unfit to stand in God's presence. Remember this important principle: broken laws lead to broken lives.

Don't put a question mark where God puts a period.

# The "Ologies" Back Up God's Orderliness

If you've studied biology, think about the examples of order God provided in DNA and molecular structure. Studies of plants and animals reveal groupings, patterns, and sequences—in other words, order.

God's examples range from tiny cellular structures to a colossal cosmic universe. **Biology and zoology—all the scientific "ologies" confirm theology**, our religious beliefs based on the Bible!

It's nice to know some things don't change. Imagine tomorrow morning you woke up from a great night's sleep only to discover gravity had gone on vacation. You would step off your bed and find you and your cell phone floating around the room.

From A to Z, anthropology to zoology, God is intimately involved with the way things work. He cares about the details of life.

"Order is heaven's first law."
—Alexander Pope (18th Century English poet)

21

# Surely Not Me?

We appreciate order when it comes to gravity and food, but there's something in us that resists when it infringes on what we want—and what we want to have control over. For instance, when I'm running late, I'd like to blow through all the traffic lights. How about you?

Circumstances and human nature work to make excuses for us to disregard staying in the "lines." We tiptoe to the edge of the sidewalk and stick our little toes on the turf because there's a sign that says, "Do not step on the grass." We tap the benches with the "wet paint" signs just to see if what they say is true. There's a saying, "Tell a man that there are 400 billion stars, and he'll believe you. Tell him a bench has wet paint, and he has to touch it." I don't know who said it, but it's true, isn't it?

Most people see the wisdom in everyone else crossing a busy street in the safety of its crosswalk. It's a different story when we're in a hurry. That gives us the privilege to be the exception to the rule, doesn't it? It's OK if we jaywalk. Never mind the fact we could cause an accident. Oh, but *we* would have it all under control—unless we dropped our purse, or lost our shoe, or tripped. What we thought would be a nice shortcut could become a dangerous, even life-threatening situation. You might think this is an insignificant example, but think about this: Without order, every intersection would be an ongoing accident scene. Order is important!

I know. I know. We're supposed to be talking about hair, right? **What does hair have to do with cells and stars and order?** We're looking at the foundation first—approaching God's Word with respect and embracing its concepts, even those we haven't yet fully understood. Remember, God didn't put mysteries in the Bible to unsettle or confuse people. The Scriptures clearly establish the necessity of women having long, uncut hair, and if we are wise we will open our hearts and analyze the Word of God (II Timothy 2:15).

You may never have known God has anything to say about hair. Perhaps you never understood what the Bible teaches on the subject. The truth is, some of the verses aren't written in language we use in our everyday conversations. You may have read I Corinthians, chapter 11, many times without understanding. My prayer for you today is that as we look into the Word and open our hearts, God will show us things we never before understood. In Luke 8:10 we see God opened the disciples' understanding to things previously unknown: "Unto you it is given to know the mysteries of the kingdom of God." That's pretty exciting—quite an honor, too. And since Jesus is the same yesterday, today, and forever, He can do it for us even now.

# What's a Mystery?

One of the definitions the dictionary gives for *mystery* is "any truth that is unknowable except by divine revelation."[4] The apostle Paul said, "I do not want you to be ignorant of this mystery, brothers" (Romans 11:25, NIV). He even said the gospel is a mystery (Ephesians 6:19). Imagine that! That's the message of salvation and eternal life! Surely God isn't playing spiritual hide-and-seek. He's not willing that any should be lost and perish.

God doesn't want the good news of the gospel hidden. Maybe He wants to see how much we're willing to invest in understanding things for ourselves, sharing with others, and growing in our faith. Jesus doesn't want you and me to stay in spiritual kindergarten.

God has gone to a lot of effort to bring us into relationship with Him, so while He is not hiding,

> God doesn't want the good news of the gospel hidden.

He is drawing us with His love. His greatest desire is that we would love Him in return—that we love Him as He loves us, with all our hearts, souls, minds, and strength (Mark 12:30). That's pretty much everything, girls—

our emotions, our eternal beings, our thoughts and understandings, and our physical abilities and resources. When we do that, oh, the treasures our spirits will experience and our spiritual eyes will see.

For now, we need to focus on growing from our initial salvation experience (instant purity) to functioning as responsible, loving believers (developing maturity). A rosebud is perfect; but God did not design it to stay a bud. When it opens, it expands and gives fragrance and beauty, then releases seeds that bless its environment. God doesn't make us mature the moment we choose to live our lives for Him. When we are born again, we are His little seeds, planted and ready to grow.

Spiritual young'uns or spiritual giants, regardless of the stage of growth we are in, |God is looking for moral excellence and purity of spirit.| When we are truly His, doing our best to follow His ways, our attitudes and characteristics will become more and more like Jesus'.

more and more like JESUS

"There are **three classes** of people:

Those who **see.**

Those who **see** when they are **shown.**

Those who do **not see.**"

—Leonardo da Vinci

Self portrait, by Leonardo da Vinci
Courtesy of Wikipedia Commons

25

# He Made the Difference

From the beginning, God created men and women with similar specifications and some distinct differences. Think about this: Without surgery, human bodies are unalterable from their original conditions. Of course, I'm not talking about losing or gaining weight, or anything temporary. Permanently, though, our bodies have their basic parts and shapes that define whether we are male or female. Our bodies, male and female, were designed by God.

There is one small feature that is changeable with ease, and that is our hair. In Revelation 9:8, the Bible identifies a certain "hair of women," and this lets us know women's hair is different from men's.

# Before the Beginning

Before God made the world, He had been in a close relationship with Satan. God called him the "anointed cherub that covereth" (Ezekiel 28:14). He was a spirit being that was beautiful, decked out in gemstones. Satan had a sweet situation in Heaven, complete with power, position, and glory, but he became proud in his beauty and corrupt in his desires. He lost focus of his purpose. He wanted to be on the same level as God (Isaiah 14:14), but he abandoned the purpose for his existence. When he did, he lost out on true beauty: reflecting God's glory in purity and holiness. He was stripped of the most important thing of all: a relationship with God.

His glory came from reflecting God's glory. When he was expelled from Heaven and the presence of God, he was not a happy camper. And he didn't go alone. That's a lesson we need to remember. When we lift our own thinking above God's ways that are higher than ours, not only do we lose out, but our choices affect others.

After Satan fell, did God have a longing in His heart for someone who would choose to love Him and be faithful to Him? Could that be why He made Adam and Eve? Could it be that this is one of the reasons God created humanity in His image—with a longing to be loved? We all want to be loved, don't we?

Perhaps Satan was jealous of Adam and Eve. It's clear he wanted to drive a wedge between them and God, so he devised a plan. He persuaded Eve to be disobedient to the rules God had made. Satan is still using this same tactic today.

# "Why Eve?" or "Why, Eve, Why?"

Think about this. God created Adam in His image, and then He created Eve from Adam's flesh. Satan focused his temptations and twisted God's word on the woman. She was the one who believed Satan's deception. Being a woman, I'd rather not think about that, but it's true, no matter if I like it or not.

But I have some **good news** to help wash down that bad news. God has given us His Spirit! It is a Holy Spirit that separates us for Him, and with His "set-apart" Spirit we can undo what was done in the Garden of Eden. It's a part of His plan. To live in the victory God has for us—and who doesn't want to live in victory?—we can't be ignorant of Satan's devices.

Eve let her guard down, and we should learn from her mistake. It's better to learn from the mistakes of others than from our own, don't you think? That's usually a lot less painful and embarrassing. My own special made-up word created for just such situations is **"humblizing."**

28

# Guard Your Garden!

There are some things it would be so much better that we didn't experience for ourselves. When we faithfully maintain our personal "gardens" with the biblical guidelines God established, we act with pure, blessed wisdom from on high. I'm talking about our lives, girls—our relationships, and our activities. Remember, God put boundaries in place because we are precious to Him and He wants to bless and protect us. As we discussed in *The Girl in the Dress*, God set guardrails along life's way to keep us safe as we journey from this life to the next. Our goal is eternal life, peace, and joy in our future home sweet home—Heaven Sweet Heaven with the King of all kings. I don't know about you, but I want to get there safe and sound.

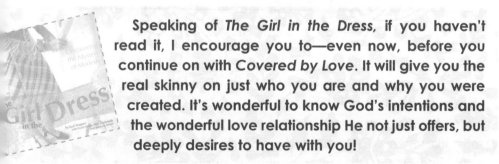

**Speaking of *The Girl in the Dress*, if you haven't read it, I encourage you to—even now, before you continue on with *Covered by Love*. It will give you the real skinny on just who you are and why you were created. It's wonderful to know God's intentions and the wonderful love relationship He not just offers, but deeply desires to have with you!**

What we wear on the outside is important and a reflection of what is in the inner person. *The Girl in the Dress* deals with both the inner and the outer person. The Bible not only tells us to dress modestly, but also to put on virtues like compassion and kindness. The things we wear—even our hair—show on the outside what's going on inside.

God's guardrails, or boundary lines, are spiritual hedges that will keep the enemy from gaining access in our lives. There are two verses I want to share with you that relate. The first one, Ecclesiastes 10:8, lays it out very simply: **"Whoso breaketh an hedge, a serpent shall bite him."** If we create openings in our hedges, we are in danger of being bitten by a snake. Notice this verse doesn't say "might" be bitten; it says "shall" bite. It's a done deal—simple math:

$$
\begin{array}{ll}
1 & \text{I break the hedge} \\
+1 & \text{the snake gets in my garden} \\
\hline
= 2 & \text{I get bitten. Yikes!}
\end{array}
$$

The other verse, Ephesians 4:27, tells us not to give place to the devil. The Greek word *topos* is the word translated *place* in this passage, and what it literally means is "ground." It's the root word for *topography*—you know, soil—like where we stand and where things grow. If we start making openings in our hedges, we clear soil or ground in our lives and make a place for the enemy to enter. He might even stick a flag in the ground and claim it for his kingdom. I don't want to see that happen to anyone!

Dear Abby,

I try to keep my hair neat and clean, but I have gotten stuck and not had time to wash my hair before I had to be somewhere. Can you give me any tips on hairdos or products that could help me through an emergency—a quick fix until I have the chance to wash it?

Jessa

Dear Jessa,

I think we've all been there before. When I'm in a situation like this, I go for a messy bun with a poof. That gets my hair off my scalp and makes its need of a wash less noticeable. All it takes is a comb, clippie, and a ponytail ring.

I've heard of some people using a bit of powder on oily spots to dry them up in an emergency situation, and there are also spray-on dry shampoos you can get at a beauty supply. These are great when you are in a pinch.

Abby

Dear Gabby,

What do you do to keep your hair healthy?

Victoria

Dear Victoria,

I know what works for me, but I think in general, it really depends on the texture of your hair. Some products work for some hair types that don't work for others. You have to learn what works best for you, and it might be a good idea to find someone who has a similar hair type and ask what they use.

Depending on a person's hair, they will use different types of products. A person with wavy hair could possibly use a cream-based hair and scalp treatment, while people with thick hair might need an oil-based treatment. When it comes to hair care, it's all about what works for you.

Gabby

## Chapter Two

# The "Covering Concept"

# The "Covering Concept"

I think we've got some great groundwork laid, and we're ready to dive into the subject of hair. I won't keep you in suspense any longer. You've been patient long enough. Really!

By the time you've finished this book, I hope you are as amazed as I am by God's intricate interweaving of what we'll call the "covering concept."

We're going to go into detail about hair, and although the topic does relate to men, this book is written for us girls. Our primary focus is the female side of the subject, but that doesn't mean hair is strictly a girly issue. It's not. Guys have their own unique instructions, and we'll touch on them—but that is a different study for another day.

## Hair Is a Covering

Hair. It's what covers our heads. The Bible specifically uses the word "covering" to describe those glorious strands sprouting from our skulls (I Corinthians 11:15). Covering is a principle we'll be looking at, but for our first example, consider the story of the wedding garment in Matthew 22:2-13. The invited guest who responded to the invitation of the king was turned away because he had no wedding garment. His fate was actually worse than being blacklisted from the season's biggest social event. He was bound up, hand and foot, and cast into outer darkness. Not good.

Why didn't he have the proper wardrobe? He received an invitation. He showed up. He wanted to go. Others had on their fine wedding threads. Surely he wasn't sporting anything as noticeably "not there" as "the emperor's new clothes"! We don't really know, but the Bible does show us through this story that what the invited guest considered "good enough" was not kosher with the king.

This parable lets us know very clearly there are acceptable and unacceptable wedding clothes. Someone might think their flip flops and frayed denim are just fine for a wedding. When someone is more concerned with her comfort or convenience than what shows appropriate respect to a gracious invitation, well, it's just rude. Rude seems to be acceptable in our society today, but it's not allowable in Heaven's courts.

This parable doesn't reveal what piece of apparel was missing. We do know that the "right" covering was mandatory to get in to the wedding. In verse 2, Jesus told us how important this parable is. It teaches us about the kingdom of Heaven—that's **eternal stuff.** Although this example speaks of one person, the verse immediately following lets us know it is an example of what will happen to the masses: "For many are called, but few are chosen" (Matthew 22:14).

As always, there's some good news to counter the bad, so here's an up-lifting verse: "I will greatly rejoice in the LORD, my soul shall be joyful in my

God; for he hath clothed me with the garments of salvation, he hath covered me with the robe of righteousness" (Isaiah 61:10). **Hang with Jesus, my friend, because He's got you covered!** We actually "put on the Lord Jesus Christ" according to Romans 13:14 (NKJV). Galatians 3:27 tells us this happens when we are baptized.

## Baptism and Covering

What does baptism have to do with hair? I told you the interweaving of the covering concept is amazing. There's much to learn in God's beautiful Word, and I hope you stay on board for the entire ride. We'll enjoy the journey as we look beyond the surface issue of "should I cut my hair or not?" In *The Girl in the Dress* we looked beyond the outer layer. We discussed how modesty is not just about the dress or clothing someone wears; it is about the girl inside the clothing. We talked about the inner person and the outer covering sending the same message to the world: we belong to Jesus. This also applies when we talk about hair. You'll see. And you'll see that hair is a covering, too.

**The name of the wisest man ever to live?**     Solomon

**What does his name mean?**     Covered

What happens when people are baptized the **biblical** way? They are covered entirely with water—from the top of their heads to the bottom of their feet. So you see, **covering** and **salvation** link together. We put on the garment of salvation when we are baptized. This all has to do with relationship, Jesus paying for our sins, our witness to the world, and becoming a part of His bride, the church.

## Unfolding Mystery

I'm telling you, girl, when you finish this book, you are going to understand some deep things. It's exciting and beautiful—like an unfolding flower. We're still at the bud stage, but it's going to be exquisite when it is fully opened.

Isn't it precious how God gives us natural examples so we can understand spiritual things we couldn't figure out on our own? He would give the story then say things like, "He who has ears, let him hear" (Matthew 11:15, NIV). What was He saying? Most everyone has ears, don't they? Jesus wasn't talking about physical perception of sound. He was talking about spiritual hearing. Dig a little deeper. Think about it and see if you can solve the puzzle and find the meaning of the mystery.

**God never told sinners to be holy (which involves being set apart for Him). He asks for separation and holiness from the people who choose to follow Him.** The truth is we won't be judged strictly on our holiness or unholiness. We will be judged first on relationship. If there is no relationship, there's no need for being set apart for God and no command for holiness. For the soul that has no relationship, there is no promise of eternity with God. For those God calls, well, He uses a different grading scale.

> "We cannot find the God of the Bible
> without following the Bible of the God."
> —Erickson Fabien

The goal shouldn't be to meet the minimum requirements to scrape into Heaven "by the hairs of our chinny chin chins" or our consecrated heads. I hope your goal is to walk as closely and pleasing to God as possible.

God has reasons for the things He asks of us. Sometimes we get to know them, and sometimes we just have to believe God enough to go with what He said. **I'm thankful for the times I "get it," but regardless of how much we understand, we are accountable to observe the instructions in His Word.**

As we grow spiritually, we gain greater understanding of God and His ways. When we were born into the kingdom of God, we were like newborn babies, and that's great. That makes the Father happy. What parent would be happy if their fully functional fifteen-year-old was still sucking her thumb, drinking from a bottle, or (Heaven forbid) wearing diapers! Yuck-o-la!

## Is "If God Said It" Enough?

Although I heartily agree with "if God said it, that's enough for me," I have to admit I really like it when I get to know the reasons behind restrictions. For instance, if I'm driving and have to stop at a barricade, I have to trust the road is blocked for a reason.

I hope you're not surprised when I tell you this relates to hair, too! Remember, **for safety's sake, don't remove the road markers unless you know why they were put there in the first place.**

I hope you trust that God knows best. I will be honest and tell you there's something in me that sometimes wants more than "because I said so." That doesn't mean I willfully choose to disobey what I don't understand, because I believe God has a purpose behind everything He says and does. Order is one of the most important reasons God wants distinction between the ways men and women appear—even their hair. **When a woman allows her hair to grow to its natural length, she wears a covering designed especially for her by God who loves her. It's a covering of love.**

We don't want to oversimplify and take extreme points of view, but we do want to be biblical in our life decisions, in our faith.

**Chapter Three**

# Hairstory
# Lessons

# Hairstory Lessons

**Let's take a little stroll through hairdo history.**

Women have had some crazy hairdos over the years. In ancient Rome, women would pile their hair into towers of curls and sprinkle them with gold dust. Sometimes they added blond hairpieces made from the hair of German captives. In Eighteenth-Century Europe, women wore headdresses up to two feet high built on top of their heads. They started with wire frames, added fake hair, coated the creation with lard, and finished it off by dusting it with flour. Women left these on for weeks, sometimes months, even though they made their heads incredibly itchy and gave off nasty smells as the lard decomposed.

**For the first 5,900 years of recorded human history, the majority of moral, God-fearing females allowed their hair to grow to God-given lengths.** It wasn't until World War I that women in the United States began cutting their hair. It happened as they began taking men's positions in factories and marked the beginning of changing roles in our society. In the Roaring Twenties, people turned from traditional roles and values to shallow amusements, immorality, and materialism. It was a breaking away from "normalcy"—a word President

Harding coined to describe the calm order prior to the rebellious decade. Note the word "order" in reference to "normalcy."

The Twenties was the beginning of a merging of genders. Songs of the day reflected the confusion. One song recorded by several artists was "Masculine Women, Feminine Men." Here are a few of the lyrics:

> Masculine women, feminine men
> Which is the rooster, which is the hen?
> Girls were girls and boys were boys when I was a tot,
> Now we don't know who is who, or even what's what!

From the lyrics of the song we see the confusion that dominated this turbulent time. The issue of "bobbed hair" caused a national uproar. Documented in one *Saturday Evening Post* article by Marian Spitzer ("The Erstwhile Crowning Glory," June 27, 1925): "There hasn't been a newspaper printed for the last two years … that hasn't carried some sort of little story … about women's hair. It used to be a woman's crowning glory, but now it's just hair."

"There hasn't been a newspaper printed for the last two years … that hasn't carried some sort of little story … about women's hair. It used to be a woman's crowning glory, but now it's just hair."

Ann Harding wrote an article for *The Ladies Home Journal* ("Your Crowning Glory," March 1927) that read: |"**The most radical change in the costume of women in our times has been the change in hair styles. Hair really is the crowning glory of a woman … her hair still remains the most telling item of her appearance.**"| Society was in an upheaval. Sadly, some men divorced their wives over the issue. Hospitals and department stores fired female employees. "By the mid 1920s, with the growing flapper craze, bobbed hair sweeps the nation. In Paducah, Kentucky, five nurses are suspended from training school for cutting their hair. … but nothing stops them—'bobbed' hair is in."[5]

Society seemed to teeter a bit and level off during the next few decades, but by the Sixties, rebellion rose again. It was a time of riots, drug use, unisex clothing, atheism, rock and roll music, and loose morals. The hippie movement was in full force—a counter-culture revolution with hair being the most obvious outward symbol of protest. It began with the shaggy-haired Beatles and was joined by young men across the nation.

During this time a rock musical, *Hair*, came out. The cast's portrayals of drug use and sexuality caused quite a stir. The show promoted the hippie lifestyle and protested things the people involved thought were wrong in America. Its profanity-filled songs became anthems, or songs of devotion. The overarching message was a challenge to any restriction society placed on their lives. Scott Miller, a theater writer, said of the musical's message that long hair "was a visible form of awareness. …The longer the hair got, the more expansive the mind was. Long hair was shocking, and it was a revolutionary act to grow long hair. It was kind of a flag, really."[6]

I have to throw my two cents in here on that comment. If long hair on men was a hippie flag flying against traditional values and morality, when we girls wear our hair long, it is a symbol of our beliefs in biblical values like purity, fidelity, and divine order.

I hope you noticed that hairstyle related to the beliefs of people who were rebelling against society or what was accepted as normal. There is definitely an association between the outer appearance and the inner state of being and belief system. After all, if it's "just hair," why is it so important? One reason is that hairstyle is a good indicator of what group of people we belong to—at least who we want to be associated with.

According to *Hairdo! What We Do and Did to Our Hair*, by Ruth Freeman Swain, "A person's hair could show what they believe in, what they cared about, and probably what music they listened to." She also said, "Hairdos have always shown a lot about who we are." To claim how we wear our hair has nothing to do with the attitudes of our hearts just doesn't seem true blue.

Notice how hair categorizes people. Hippies and metalheads have long hair. Punkers love their Mohawks and other spikey and dyed styles. Then there's the deathhawk, a bigger back-combed version of the Mohawk favored by Goths and deathrock fans. Cybergoths tend to go for the undercuts—shaving the sides and back of their heads and allowing the top to grow long. We can't forget the Emo crowd who favors very short hair with a long side fringe, often dyed black or some crazy non-hair color.

How about those monks? They have their own unique hairdos called "tonsure," and when you see one, you know they didn't pick that to say, "I'm in fashion." They do it because of their religious beliefs. Just what is a "military cut"? How can we give a haircut a name like that if it doesn't associate us with a group of people? In my day people got the "Dorothy Hamill" or the "Farrah Fawcett," while today girls flock into salons to copy current stars' latest dos.

## Bible Study Time!

Now that we've had a look at secular history, let's take a look in God's history book—the Holy Bible. A very compact, to-the-point teaching on hair is found in I Corinthians 11. As we've already discussed, the concept of covering began in the Garden and continues to the great wedding day in Heaven. Let's look at what Paul taught the Corinthian church on the subject. Keep in mind that Paul wasn't giving a new set of ideas—a modernized, progressive word to just one group of people in their particular situation. He was restating timeless, universal principles already laid in the foundational writings of the Old Testament. In the same letter, he instructed those reading it to, "acknowledge that what I am writing to you is the Lord's command" (I Corinthians 14:37, NIV).

> "There is a craze these days to hear
> something new from the Lord;
> But what we need to hear are those things we
> have heard all along, but have not listened to."
> — Oswald Chambers

First we need to address a few questions. It's not wrong, by the way, to have questions. Sometimes people question because they really want to believe. I hope that's you!

Paul worked eighteen months to establish a church in the city of Corinth (Acts 18:11). After he left, serious problems broke out. Paul was actively involved in the leadership and growth of the churches he established.

God gave Paul and the other apostles authority to handle the challenges the new church faced—with timeless, God-given principles. Paul taught that they should do things God's way, regardless of the wickedness of their environment or the choices others made.

What was going on in the church? Its membership included people on both ends of the spectrum in their beliefs. They were all new converts—from rule-following Jews to those who believed a doctrine of freewill and self-government called libertarians. On one hand there were people raised with strong teaching in the Old Testament, and on the other hand were people accustomed to the "free" society of Corinth. Everyone brought his or her background and old beliefs with them into the church. Paul was trying to get them to a place of balance in respecting God's divine, holy order.

"To obey God is perfect liberty." —Seneca

Now we know who wrote the book and why— and a bit about the Corinthians. That's good, but were Paul's writings just for that local church for their brief blip on history's radar screen? We don't have the letter Paul received from the Corinthians, but we do know he was writing in direct response to questions they asked (I Corinthians 7:1). If we embrace the teachings of the rest of the letter on love, it only makes sense these words are for our benefit as well.

In I Corinthians, chapter 11, Paul deals with a cultural issue that was a problem. He is setting the record straight so they will know what God expects of them. Look at how Paul begins the letter: "To the church of God in Corinth, to those sanctified in Christ Jesus and called to be holy, together with all those everywhere who call on the name of our Lord Jesus Christ—their Lord and ours" (I Corinthians 1:2, NIV). Paul's own words tell us he is not writing solely to the Corinthians, but to all those everywhere who call on the name of Jesus! That's you and me, and believers in Kalamazoo and Timbuktu. **The principles Paul taught the Corinthians were timeless and relevant to every culture.**

Let's see what the passage says. We'll use the New International Version to simplify the language.

[1] *Follow my example, as I follow the example of Christ.*

[2] *I praise you for remembering me in everything and for holding to the teachings, just as I passed them on to you.*

[3] *Now I want you to realize that the head of every man is Christ, and the head of the woman is man, and the head of Christ is God.*

[4] *Every man who prays or prophesies with his head covered dishonors his head.*

[5] *And every woman who prays or prophesies with her head uncovered dishonors her head—it is just as though her head were shaved.*

[6] *If a woman does not cover her head, she should have her hair cut off; and if it is a disgrace for a woman to have her hair cut or shaved off, she should cover her head.*

*7 A man ought not to cover his head, since he is the image and glory of God; but the woman is the glory of man.*

*8 For man did not come from woman, but woman from man;*

*9 Neither was man created for woman, but woman for man.*

*10 For this reason, and because of the angels, the woman ought to have a sign of authority on her head.*

*11 In the Lord, however, woman is not independent of man, nor is man independent of woman.*

*12 For as woman came from man, so also man is born of woman. But everything comes from God.*

*13 Judge for yourselves: Is it proper for a woman to pray to God with her head uncovered?*

*14 Does not the very nature of things teach you that if a man has long hair, it is a disgrace to him,*

*15 But that if a woman has long hair, it is her glory? For long hair is given to her as a covering.*

*16 If anyone wants to be contentious about this, we have no other practice — nor do the churches of God.*

There's more to this chapter. It goes on to talk about communion (remember that), but we'll stop here for now and dive in to what we've read. The first two verses instruct the church to follow Paul as he follows God and to hold on to the things he had already taught them. Through his letter, perhaps he wanted to give them some of the reasons why.

Verse 3 connects with verse 2. I'm sure you learned in an English lesson the word "but" is a conjunction—it acts like a coupler joining two train cars. Paul is saying to hang on to the traditions—*and* there is something more. The King James Version translates it "I would have you to know."

The word "head" is used in more than one way in this chapter. In verse 3, when it's referring to who is head over the other, it means the one in charge. *Strong's Concordance* says "head" is a metaphor (comparison) for anything supreme, chief, or prominent.[7] Think of a totem pole that has an order from top to bottom—one "head" on top of the other in vertical order.

Now let's look at verses 4-6. This is where the "heads" can get confusing. A man who prays or prophesies with his physical head covered dishonors his spiritual head: Jesus. A woman who prays or prophesies with her physical head uncovered dishonors her spiritual head. Paul said if she does this, it's the same as if she shaved her head. He goes on to tell us in verse 6 "if," or "since," it is a disgrace to have her hair cut off or shaved, she should cover her head.

We're ready to move on to verse 10. The NIV begins it with "therefore," but let's look at it in the King James:

"For this cause ought the woman to have power on her head because of the angels." Whether we begin the passage with "therefore" or "for this cause," we are referred back to the verse before. Therefore, because of what, or for what cause, is Paul referring to? We get the answer from verse 9: because of God's established order regarding male-female relationships. And what should women do for this cause or reason? We should be covered. Why? To have power and because of the angels. From this passage we learn that a girl who is not "covered" is missing out on spiritual power. I don't know about you, but I can use all the help I can get.

Let's break verse 10 down so we can understand it better, but first I am going to have to give you a sneak peek into verse 15: "long hair is given to her as a covering." It's God's plan, and girls, it's not right to put our ideas and desires above God's. When we willingly submit to God's plan, we reveal our acceptance of our distinct functions and roles by being covered when we pray or prophesy. In I Thessalonians 5:17, we are instructed to pray without ceasing. Having a nonstop covering as we daily maintain attitudes of prayer helps us fulfill this biblical instruction.

**A woman's outer covering reveals an inner acceptance of God's plan.** By her conduct, of her own free will, she gains power on her head. The visible, highly noticeable symbol of long hair a woman wears shows she is honoring her head, which in turn empowers her with her own authority.

You may not care about power or authority. As the song says, "Girls just wanna have fun." I'm all for fun, and I don't want to dim one little flicker of your sparkler, but life's not just about fun.

|We need strength and insight to help us through this world and into the next.|

> "There are two freedoms:
> The false where one is free to do what he likes
> and the true where he is free to do what he ought."
> —Charles Kingley

Let's look at some specific word meanings to help us understand some key points. In verse 6 we read it is a disgrace for a woman to have her hair cut off or shaved. The word "disgraced" in the NIV is translated "shame" in the King James. This word comes from the Greek word *aischron* from the root word *aischros* which means "filthy." I found it amazing that it also means "disfigurement." It makes sense that if we cut our bodies, we disfigure them, but I never thought about cutting hair in the same way—disfigurement. These are strong words, my sister. They are not mine but the literal meanings of the words of the Bible. The more I ponder it, the more I think I'd rather be graced than disgraced!

Of course, as with all God's invitations, we have a choice to make, but think about it. **The choice to allow our hair to grow connects us with glory, power, and angels. The choice to cut our hair is associated with disfigurement, disgrace, shame, or filth.** It's our choice, and I Corinthians 11:10 gives us a good reason to choose covering. The woman who chooses to submit to God's divine order, and shows that by not cutting her hair, has power on her head.

## Power on Her Head

What does it mean to "have power on her head"? According to *Strong's Concordance*, the word "on" in the phrase "on her head" could be translated "of position."[8] The woman has power of position when she is in her God-ordained place. When we display God's order to the world through our covering of hair, power, glory, and honor are ours. **When we keep our hair, we keep our position.** It is a privilege not to be taken lightly. We also give the world an important spiritual illustration.

A woman's joyful acceptance of her role in God's kingdom is an example to the world of the relationship between Jesus and His church. A proper hair covering shows proper relationship. It is a recognition that **woman was made for man the same way humankind was made for God. She is a treasured but weaker vessel—an object of love to be cherished.**

This does not mean a man has a higher value than a woman. Paul nips that wrong thinking right in the bud

object of love

in verse 11.

The *King James* puts
it this way: "Nevertheless
neither is the man without the woman,
neither the woman without the man, in the Lord."
The fact is, we all come from God. Women would be extinct without men, and men would be extinct without women. It looks like as far as God is concerned, the dependency men and women have on each other creates an equal value.

We're down to verse 13: "Judge for yourselves: Is it proper for a woman to pray to God with her head uncovered?" We'll talk about the judging aspect a bit later, but what is to be judged? Is it proper for a woman to pray with her head uncovered? Paul didn't ask the question because he didn't know the answer. He asked the question to get people to think about the subject themselves. Then he gives more things to think about.

In verse 14 we are asked to consider that even nature tells us it's not right for a man to have long hair. The word *nature* in this verse actually refers to "the nature of things," "the order of nature," and is "opposed to that which is … abnormal, perverse."[9] Doesn't nature teach us that long hair on a woman is her glory?

There are some things we can be certain of. Although the covering mentioned in verse 6 may not be clearly defined, verse 15 tells us, without question, long hair is given to a woman as a covering. Who gave it to her? God!

Remember we're using the NIV for readability, but for finding the original intent of a complicated passage, I go to classic KJV and other more strict translations and study helps. Sometimes in modernizing the language for translation, the impact of the message is weakened. Let's look at the end of verse 6. Where the NIV says "she should cover her head," both the *King James* and *Young's Literal Translations* say she must "be covered." The *Young's Literal Translation* gives us more information in verse 15: "the hair instead of a covering hath been given to her."

According to verse 15, long hair is a girl's glory given for her covering—a covering of love. We choose how we handle the glorious covering He's given us. Will we wear it as a crown of honor or cast it to the floor to be swept in the dustpan with the dirt and debris of the world? Oh, my.

## Sticky Stuff

Now let's look at some of the sticky words. Oh, yes, they are in there, and we're going to deal with them. Some people argue verse 15 is not a direct command. It does, after all, say, "*if* a woman has long hair." Yes, it does. God continues to allow people their free wills, but think about this. The word *glory* in this verse is the same word translated for the majesty of God that filled the Tabernacle in the wilderness

(Hebrews 9:5). It also refers to the radiance and splendor that fills Heaven's throne room (Revelation 15:8). According to *Thayer's Lexicon*, it also means "on whom the divine glory rests." [10] It's our choice to make, but I'm thrilled for the opportunity to wear a covering of long hair. When we make this choice, we become one "on whom the divine glory rests." Let's go for the glory, girls!

Some questions on this passage of Scripture can be answered by the footnotes of the 1984 NIV translation: "Every man who prays or prophesies with long hair dishonors his head. And every woman who prays or prophesies with no covering of hair on her head dishonors her head—she is just like one of the 'shorn women.' If a woman has no covering, let her be for now with short hair, but since it is a disgrace for a woman to have her hair shorn or shaved, she should grow it again. A man ought not to have long hair" (I Corinthians 11:4-7, NIV footnotes). [11]

Notice that Paul did not want women leading in public worship if they were not covered. This is not a denominational issue mandated by Paul, or by current-day pastors. It's a New Testament standard to keep order in the church.

I confess. I've had a bad hair day a time or two, and I've wondered if keeping my hair long was worth the trouble I was experiencing at the moment. That brings us to another question. Is this really *necessary*? After all, in I Corinthians 11:10, Paul said a woman "ought," not "must," have long hair. The Greek word for ought, *opheil* , means "to owe," "to be in debt for," or "that which is due." So the answer to the question is another question: **Will we choose to give God that which is due?**

Define "long." God is so good. He places us all on an equal footing when it comes to "long." You see, some girls' hair physically can't grow more than a few inches, and others might have Rapunzelitis (from the fairy tale story). If "long" meant inches, we could get caught up in judging spirituality by hair length.

The Greek word for "long hair" in verses 14 and 15 doesn't have anything to do with measurement. A measurement is a noun, like inches or centimeters. The Greek word *koma* is a verb that means "to let the hair grow." If long is a verb, that means it is an action word—something that is happening continually. If we allow our hair to grow, that obviously means we aren't shortening it in any fashion—cutting, shaving, or otherwise. It's impossible to cut your hair and let it grow at the same time.

> "'Long' is not measured in inches, but obedience."
> —Scott Graham

"Long hair" is not a thing for a girl to achieve, but an active, ongoing growth—something that can be seen. It's a continual condition in the same way guys continually maintain their short hair.

**Long hair is a girl's visual "amen" or "so be it" to her inner acceptance of God's desire for gender distinction—a banner of love.**
I look at it this way:

- ♥ I am God's girl doing things His way. My hair says, "Amen!"
- ♥ I'm lined up in right relationship with God and men. My hair says, "Amen!"
- ♥ I live in God's divine order in the presence of angels—and that gives me power! My hair says, "Amen!"
- ♥ When temptations come to cut my hair, I'm not going to listen. My hair just says, "Amen!"
- ♥ You and I may not fully understand everything about covering, but we know enough about this biblical principle that makes it worth living out. For those who experience the blessing and power that come when we follow God's directives, I have this to say. Ladies, we have to hold on to what God has given us! And about those "bad hair days"—I had more of them before I made the commitment to allow my hair to grow.

Let's wrap up this look at I Corinthians 11. First, remember we are dealing with more than one standalone verse that seeks to stifle and control women. It's really quite the opposite. If we look at Paul's writings as a whole, we see he acknowledged the roles of women in the church. He sent his greetings to them in his letters. He worked alongside them in ministry. Some might call Paul a chauvinist, but what we really see in this chapter is an in-depth explanation from an impassioned apostle at an overarching biblical principle. The long and short of the matter breaks down into two categories and seems a simple choice to make:

## 1 Uncut Hair

Honor
Covering
Power
Angels
Glory

## 2 Cut Hair

Dishonor
Shame

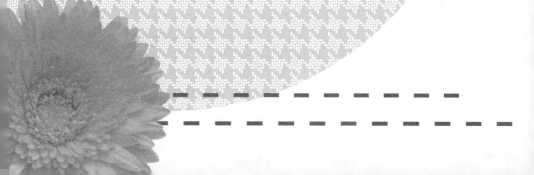

## Chapter Four

# Looking Back to Look Forward

# Looking Back to Look Forward

Have you ever studied the Tabernacle in the wilderness? You might agree with me it's an interesting subject but are probably wondering how—oh how—is she going to relate this to hair?

Humans primarily think in timelines, but God lives way beyond—outside any box we could put Him in. Things happen in the here and now, and in the way back then, that relate to things outside time.

Let's take a look back through time at the Ark of the Covenant. When I think of the Ark, I think of the golden box God commanded Moses to have built when He gave directions for the Tabernacle. This was after God saved the Israelites from slavery in Egypt (Exodus 29:46). You know what is so cool about every aspect of the Tabernacle, including the Ark? They were made during a certain time in our world but were copies of things that already existed outside of time in Heaven (Hebrews 8:5). That's mind blowing!

You and I—our brains think in a straight timeline. We move back in time to think about the Ark and the Tabernacle, but they are shadows of things already made in Heaven. That's pretty important.

We've talked a lot about order. Remember, it's a biblical principle. When we look at Tabernacle order, we will see wonderful relationship, glory, angels, and covering. It's so exciting! The Tabernacle may well be a sort of "map key" that helps us unlock spiritual mysteries.

# Tabernacle Order

"Covering" is a major topic of the Tabernacle. God wanted a Tabernacle as an established meeting place for Him and mankind—like the Garden and Adam and Eve. It was their "special place," their rendezvous point. Remember how Adam and Eve sinned and polluted paradise? Our holy and just God couldn't be in close relationship with people marred by sin. Because He still loved them, He put a plan in place to make things right—**a bridge of love.** God made a way for sinners to be restored to the God Who loved them.

Here's one of my favorite verses: "Mercy and truth are met together; righteousness and peace have kissed each other" (Psalm 85:10). Isn't that sweet? I love that verse! It tells us so much about the heart of God—of His desire for us and His passion. This meeting—this kissing of mercy and truth—is exactly what happened in the Tabernacle.

Let's take a look at the Tabernacle. From the outside, the first thing we would see is a fence 150 feet long and 75 feet wide. It was made of finely woven linen and created an enclosed courtyard. There was only one entrance, the gate, and once you were inside, there was a very particular order in which things were arranged.

Once inside the gate, the first thing you ran into was the place of repentance—the altar of sacrifice or literally "slaughter place." It was a large square structure with a ramp leading up to it where animals and produce were offered for different sacrifices. It was a place where blood and coals were collected for use elsewhere.

Directly after the altar was a huge laver, or basin—like a sink, but without the tap and plug. It was shiny, made from the mirrors Jewish women donated, and was used by the priests primarily for washing after the sacrifices. When the priests looked in the reflection on the water, they saw what needed washing. This is a picture of the bride of Christ cleansed by the washing of the Word (Ephesians 5:26). On a side note, ladies, cleanliness is important—inside and out. The Bible points out what needs washing on the inside the same way natural mirrors show us the spinach stuck between our teeth. It's something that needs to happen on a regular basis. Just look to the priests for that example. Daily sacrifices were followed by daily cleansing.

Now we've looked at everything in the courtyard. Most of Israel was not allowed beyond this point, only the priests. As members of the new covenant, we are part of a "royal priesthood" (I Peter 2:9), a "holy priesthood" (I Peter 2:5), and we have access to the Tabernacle's most sacred chamber. Good things happened in the courtyard, but God doesn't want us to hang around outside the Holy Place. Everything done in the courtyard was done in preparation to enter the Tabernacle, a special "covered place" also known as the Holy of Holies.

The Tabernacle was carefully covered—a very special place that told of the coming relationship Jesus will have with His bride, the church. It had four

unique coverings that created a rectangular tent separated into two compart-
ments by a veil. The outer covering was made of what the *King James Bible*
calls badger skins. The old word translated "badger" doesn't refer to what we
know as badgers in North America. Bible scholars believe it was a form of ma-
rine life—probably the dugongs that grazed along the shores of the Red Sea.

I'd never heard of a dugong before I studied this out—but isn't it fun to
say? Dugong. Dugong. Dugong. What are dugongs? They are mammals born
with thick, creamy skin that darkens to brownish or gray over time. Their
barrel-shaped bodies are sparsely covered in short hair, and they can get
quite large—over six hundred pounds. Their skins would have provided a
fairly waterproof outer covering for the Tabernacle. I couldn't help noticing
the resemblance of the dugong's skin to human flesh.

Under the outer skin covering was another covering also made of skins.
These were from rams and they were dyed red. As I studied, I began to see
a picture unfolding—a person with red blood circulating beneath
the outer skin covering.

Curtains made of goats' hair made the
next level of covering. Goats' hair? Yes. And
is there any significance to that? I thought so
when I recalled the Bible compares human
hair to goats' hair (I Samuel 19:13; Song of
Solomon 4:1). Solomon said long, flowing hair

resembled a flock of goats on a mountain. So we see skin, blood, and hair. What's next?

The final covering was made of fine linen embroidered with cherubim (angels) in beautiful blue, scarlet, and purple (Exodus 26:1-6). This is the covering the priests saw as they ministered inside the Holy Place. Everywhere they looked, angels seemed to float in these curtains that lined the ceiling and walls of the Tabernacle.

Cherubim have been in the presence of God since before the time of the Garden of Eden. Satan was the "anointed cherub that covereth." Cherubim are even now with God in Heaven, and it was the Lord's instructions that images of them be woven into the Tabernacle's curtains. There's more to come on these special angels, but for now, I hope you get the beautiful picture the Tabernacle gives. **It's a picture of Heaven and communion with God which includes the presence of angels beneath a holy, sacred covering.** It's an illustration of Heaven on earth—and there's order in the court of the King!

> The truth is, there's no quick answer to the hair question. If all you wanted was "it's in the Bible," you wouldn't be reading this book. Hang on. We're walking through the complicated now, but we'll get to the simple—because it all boils down to simple concepts of covering and order.

We're now ready to walk inside the Tabernacle. In the first room are three items: a golden candlestick, a table with special bread on it called "shewbread," and an altar for offering prayers and incense. These were set in a specific order. The first, **the golden candlestick**, stood to the left of the en-

trance. It represented the Spirit of God and had to be maintained daily so its light would never go out.

**The table of shewbread**, to the right of the Tabernacle door, was a place to simply show bread. Twelve loaves represented the twelve tribes of Israel and remained continually before the Lord. They indicated the never-ending relationship between God and His people. Priests ate the shewbread from the table after they replaced it with new bread each week.

The last item in the first room, the altar of incense, was located directly in front of the veil to the Most Holy Place. Priests prayed there every morning and evening. Once a year, on the Day of Atonement, the high priest sprinkled blood on the altar before removing his outer robes and entering the Most Holy Place.

The Tabernacle, which God set up as a pattern, is a straight path to the presence of the Lord. It's like an arrow pointing from the wilderness, through the gate, stopping at all the points along the way, and directing us into the private inner chamber. This is the place God spiritually connected with ordinary men. It reminds me of Esther. She was just a common girl and not worthy according to worldly standards to be queen, but she was the one chosen by the king.

The curtain dividing the two rooms of the Tabernacle represented further separation and increased holiness. Only the high priest entered this sacred chamber where humanity and deity met. Behind the curtain, or veil, was one piece of furniture: **the golden Ark of the Covenant.** The Ark was covered with a top called the Mercy Seat that had two golden cherubim carved on either side. These angels had their wings raised and folded over, and looked to the covering—the place where the glory of God sat on the Mercy Seat. Key point: angels, glory, covering, holy place, communion with God—all in the covered place of atonement. When I read this, it sent me straight to I Corinthians 11.

# Atonement? What's That?

Let's stop right here and look at the word "atonement" and how that applies to hair and covering. Covering is a spiritual principle. We can only enter the presence of the Lord when we are covered in His righteousness—His atonement. What exactly is "atonement"? That's a fifty-cent word most people don't use every day, but what it means is "at-one-ment." **Atonement means covering and implies being "at one" with God.** The greatest covering of all is the one Jesus provided for His bride, the church (II Corinthians 5:21). He became a sin offering so we could be made the righteousness of God in Him. *In Him* means we are covered. When we are in Him, God doesn't see our sins; He sees the covering Jesus provided for us. It's like this. If I'm in my car, you don't really see me. I'm in there, but I'm covered in boring green minivan (ugh). We can't roll into Heaven unless we're covered in Christ. That's atonement.

There are many types of covering in the Bible. It is an overarching concept that began before creation and is carried into many aspects of this life and into the next. That's why I say it's complicated, but simple.

Because of love, God stretched out a canopy, a covering over the earth even before He made Adam and Eve (Genesis 1:6). He made them in His image, clothed in glory. **From the beginning He has covered what is special to Him. Covering sets apart and protects what God calls His.**

When it comes to covering and you and me, here's the key: **The need for covering began with sin.** It originated with disobedience to God's authority. Every aspect of covering goes back to this concept. Think about it. Adam and Eve walked in purity before the Lord. There was no need for covering sin or covering nakedness. Through their disobedience they broke relationship and required covering. Their actions were like stepping out from an umbrella into howling winds and rain. **When we accept the covering for sin offered by Jesus, we accept the restoration of God's authority in our lives.** We're not Egyptian slaves, and we're not wandering in the wilderness. We belong to Him.

Notice when we talk about covering we're referring to a canopy or an umbrella. God's not walking around Heaven with a club in His hand waiting for us to fall so He can throw us out like a moldy mixture of last week's leftovers. His covering is a shelter, like an umbrella—designed to protect, not a club—to beat into submission.

## |God's covering is a result of His love.|

If we feel the urge to step outside our "covering" (God's established order for creation), we should prayerfully consider our motives. What is feeding our impulses to do things our own way—and what direction is the path of self-will leading? I don't want to follow Mother Eve's footsteps on the path that leads to loss and separation from God.

> "Order my steps in thy word:
> and let not any iniquity have dominion over me."
> —Psalm 119:133

Atonement. Yes, it is a word we don't always "get" in our day, but being covered and "at-one" with God is a central theme of the Bible. Atonement not only means "to cover," it also means "reconcile" and "forgive." And this is really interesting. The word used for the atonement sacrifice offered in the Tabernacle is the same word used for the pitch or asphalt covering that sealed Noah's ark.[12] That's something to think about, isn't it? Those saved, those accepted by God, were covered, atoned. Atonement is a covering given by God because of His love, to bring back into grace the disgraced.

# Angels All Around

Oh, to be in the presence of the Lord is such a sweet experience! There's a "secret place" accessible to each of us. It's our own place of communion with God, as individual as each snowflake. You may not have thought about this before, but when you are alone in your secret place with God, you really aren't alone. You see, it's a place of spiritual connection, and where God is, His angels are, too.

The high priest wasn't alone in the Most Holy Place. God hung out between the cherubim on the Mercy Seat (Psalm 80:1). Angels "floated" in front, in back, on the sides, and overhead, woven in the curtains of their special place. Where God's glory met with men, under the Tabernacle coverings, angels were everywhere—a cloud of witnesses hovering all around the glory of God.

There's something special going on here. I'm getting excited just thinking about it. The Bible says when Jesus died, the veil that kept people from entering into the Holy Place was torn. God opened the door through His death and invited us into a most sacred, wonderful place.

I love Holy Ghost goosebumps—the kind I get when there's something exciting in the spiritual atmosphere. There are other goosebump moments in life, too—scary ones. You've probably heard Psalm 34:7: "The angel of the Lord encampeth round about them that fear him, and delivereth them." When we live God-honoring lives, approaching the Lord in His divine order, in times of crisis we don't have to wait for angels to show up. They are already there. They are camped out around the people who love and respect God.

As I thought about that verse one day, I began to wonder, *If the angel of the Lord camps around the people that fear Him and delivers them, what kind of angels camp around those who don't fear God? Do those who don't honor Him and His ways attract fallen angels?* Fallen angels are demonic spirits.

Yikes! That made me want to show as much honor and respect for God as possible. I can say I love God all I want, but my conduct speaks louder than words. I need to honor Him, so this great cloud of witnesses, the angels of the Lord, set up

CoNduct SpeaKs LoUder tHaN WordS.

their campsites right next to me and mine. One of the ways I do this is through my acceptance of God's divine order in my life through the physical example of my uncut hair.

While we're talking about angels, think about this. We have been saved by God's grace, but there is no hope for fallen angels. The Bible tells us angels desire to look into the things concerning salvation (I Peter 1:10-12). All angels are watching—the fallen and the faithful. They look into our lives. If women and men look the same in their outer appearances, what visible example would we show of our honor to God and His ways? What symbol will we display to angels, or the world for that matter? Of course, our character and spirit are most important, but what's on the inside should show up on the outside and be easily seen.

"You can observe a lot by watching."
—Yogi Berra

If angels rejoice when one person repents (Luke 15:10), we can keep them doing the happy dance as they watch us living in agreement with God's design! I hope as we've discussed the subject of angels, redemption, and order, the phrase "because of the angels" in I Corinthians 11:10 is beginning to be less cloudy. I trust that some of the mystery is being revealed and you're seeing things with new understanding.

I don't know about you, but I don't want to displease God or His angels. Angels know sin won't go unpunished and that sin-stained people have no right to enter God's presence. The high priest would not have dared enter the Most Holy Place without making sure everything was done exactly as God outlined. He took care to do things according to God's orders, and God's people should take the same care today. Yes, we are blessed to have constant access to the throne of grace, but that doesn't mean we should take the honor lightly. We need to respect the invisible ranks and organization God has established.

When godly, covered women enter worship, the glory of God fills the house. I hope you have experienced that heavenly presence. God's holy angels are attracted to glory—at least they are always hanging around the glory when we read about it in the Bible. Maybe that's another reason for that "because of the angels" phrase. Glory on head equals angel magnet.

## God's Visual Lesson

A woman's hair is undeniably called a covering, and without a doubt should be allowed to grow freely. God has given His girls a physical symbol to wear—a walking "visual"—like a teacher uses to get a point across.

In this visual lesson, women represent the bride of Christ, the covered, atoned, loved one clothed in righteousness. Men represent the sinless groom. Remember, women were made for men the same way mankind was made for God—for a loving, intimate relationship. Girls, we are privileged to wear the covering—a symbol to the world of redemption and God's plan for all humanity. Christian women have the honor of representing Jesus' beautiful gift of atonement for sin. Wow.

I could disregard I Corinthians 11, cut my hair, and wear a t-shirt with a cross on it, but it's just not the same. That's a mixed message and one that doesn't say "I'm God's girl, walking in His ways."

Did you ever sing "I Give Myself Away" or "I Surrender All" at church? I have. While we're standing at the altar feeling the presence of God, we think we mean the words—until we are tested on them. How much "self" are we willing to give to God? "Self" is my identity, my character, my individuality. When I looked up *self* in the thesaurus, it had related words like earthly-minded and selfish. It even listed Bible-type words like licentious (immoral), covetous (greedy), and worldly (concerned with material values or ordinary life rather than a spiritual existence). When you and I say, "I give myself to You, Lord," just how much self are we really talking about? Hair is a major indicator of our personalities, the "self" we project to the world. Are we willing to give that to God—to project His image rather than ours?

How much will we really surrender? When I think of surrender, I think of waving a white flag on the battlefield. When someone surrenders, they give up their rights and place themselves in the hands of the victor. That could be scary, for sure, if we weren't talking about putting ourselves in the hands of our loving God. God watches over us, provides for us, and wants what's best for us! It sounds like a sweet deal to me.

Submission goes against what "self" wants because it looks beyond the momentary satisfaction of feeling like I'm in control. It sees with eyes that hunger for Him more than doing things my own way based on what I think or feel. When we submit to God, like the battlefield captive waving the white flag, it means we surrender our personal rights—even our personal "fights." That's not a bad thing, my friend. When we surrender to God's divine order, we connect with something much deeper and more fulfilling than being the top dog of the heap. Some day that heap is going to rot or melt away. When I connect with the eternal in unity with God's plan, I get a sense of being more than just who I am. **When I'm just mine, I'm not very much, but when I am His, I'm so much more.**

It's easy to think of surrendering in a negative way, unless you're the victor, of course. With God, the battle is very different. When we surrender to Jesus, we are victorious *with* Him! God doesn't humiliate us or parade us around in chains like trophies. Instead, see a picture of Him reaching down to you, pulling you on His white horse behind him, and riding off in the middle of your enemies. Your white flag transforms into a banner of victory flying high as you gallop off to the castle for a grand celebration. Jesus does not fight against us. He fights for us, and then, once we're on His team, He fights with us!

The apostle Paul told servants of the Lord to teach: "In meekness instructing those that oppose themselves; if God peradventure will give them repentance to the acknowledging of the truth; and that they may recover themselves out of the snare of the devil, who are taken captive by him at his will" (II Timothy 2:25-26).

There are two things I want you to notice here. First, people can actually oppose themselves! That means you and I can be our own enemies. Second, it's the job of our spiritual leaders to teach us to turn from any wrong ways and beliefs. For our good, they want us to acknowledge the truth and come to our senses so we can escape the devil's trap. He really wants to take us captive, and not for any good reason. **If I have to be a captive, I want to be captured by God's love!**

So while "surrender" isn't always a word with a positive associated meaning, like "home" or "pumpkin spice latte" are to me, it has very positive results! Surrender is giving up—no more fighting—you win; but it also means to yield. When I think of yielding, I think of driving down the road and having to stop for traffic that has the right of way. Girls, Jesus always has the right of way, and yielding to Him isn't too hard when we get to follow His taillights all the way to Heaven!

This example takes us right back to order. There's an order to driving, and there's an order on the highway to Heaven. We are all traveling our individual roads, and they come with some road markers. Think about a four-way stop. Who gets to go first? The one who gets there first. The first driver sets the order. Well, my friends, God arrived at the intersection before any of us. He sets the order, and we follow. God's on the road. His unchanging Word is trucking along like a loaded semi rolling down Mount Elbert. If we're driving in the little hybrid of our own ideas, the really smart thing to do is yield the right of way.

YIELD

When we yield to God, we not only bless our lives, we bless the lives of those around us. That includes the people who care so very much for us: our families, our brothers and sisters in the church, and our pastors. I hope you want to bless your pastor who carries such a heavy load of responsibility. Pastors have to answer to God for the way they lead their congregations. Let's be helpful. Let's encourage one another and invite the supernatural into our natural worlds in ways that bring comfort and strength to our homes, churches, and communities. We each have a part to play, a way we can contribute. Not making waves for the pastor to fight against as he works the nets and tends to fishing is a great blessing to the kingdom of God. We have the opportunity to bless our churches. By living in harmony with God's beautiful plans, we contribute to an open environment for the Spirit to move instead of bottlenecking and damming the flow.

We live in a time when God doesn't normally show up in visible clouds of glory. He has given His Spirit to His church. We are His tabernacles, His tents—He lives in us (I Corinthians 6:19). We are the presence of God in the world—modern-day Holy Places. We have all that was in the Old Testament Tabernacle and more! We have covering. When we obey His plan, we live in the presence of glory and angels in sweet communion with God. God's natural order lived out in our lives is a witness to the world in which we live. **We are part of His creation that testifies of Him.**

Think about this. A lady's hair is her covering. Hair has no power in itself, but it does give us that symbol we talked about before, that we are in correct relationship with God. We have received redemption—Jesus' payment for our sins. We are living in agreement with His Word and ways, and that affects our lives and even angels. Our hair is a visual sign of relationship with God. I don't want to cut that relationship off!

You may think I'm being silly, but look at it this way. If I had a picture of something special to you and I cut it up right in front of you, you might feel a bit insulted. It certainly wouldn't make you feel honored, would it? Once we realize the significance of covering, and its effect on our spiritual environment, cutting it off just doesn't seem the best choice—the God-honoring choice.

## Judge for Yourself and Judge Yourself

OK. Let's move on. Some people accuse those who believe and live out the principle of covering of being judgmental. It's quite humbling to think God has given us this privilege. I don't want to point my finger at someone who hasn't been as blessed as I am to know this precious truth. So let's make sure to check our attitudes at all times.

Looking back at the Tabernacle again, the priest had to judge himself before he entered the presence of God. Speaking of judging and hair, remember what Paul said: "Judge among yourselves: Is it proper for a woman to pray to God with her head uncovered?"

> We can have long hair and not be very spiritual. Our spirits must be right or our outward appearance will not be an authentic witness.

(I Corinthians 11:13, NKJV). Paul wasn't afraid to ask the tough questions, and he was not afraid of the answers. He laid the entire case out like a high-paid attorney. And if all that wasn't enough, the very next words following the teaching we looked at in I Corinthians 11 sealed it: "If anyone wants to be contentious about this, we have no other practice—nor do the churches of God" (I Corinthians 11:16, NIV).

There's another important spiritual concept I want you to understand. We should judge ourselves and how we are maturing spiritually by how close we are to God's Word. The closer we get to God, the closer we get to His Word. We know the Ark of the Covenant, angels, and glory were in the Holy Place, but think about what was inside the Ark of the Covenant. The closer the high priest got to the presence of God, the closer he got to the Word of God written by Moses and placed inside. It doesn't seem logical to me that a person would claim to be getting more spiritual as they take steps away from biblical teaching. **As we draw nearer to His presence, we come closer to His Word.**

That said, it's also true that in today's world, so many people don't know what the Bible teaches about hair. While we're talking about judging, I caution you to be careful not to judge another person on this issue. We are blessed, my sisters, and we don't always know where others are spiritually. We aren't always able to tell if someone has lost hair because of injury or illness or some little kid went after them with toenail scissors while they were sleeping. We can't look inside hearts and see if someone has made a commitment to let their hair grow, even if their hair has obviously been cut. Once someone makes that commitment, in God's eyes, they have begun the unending process of allowing their hair to grow. They are covered from that day forward. Remember, "long" is a verb not measured in inches but by obedience—from the first day you make the commitment and every day following. The most important one to judge is yourself; and when you do, judge yourself against the teachings of the Word, not the suggestions of the world.

The Bible tells us that love covers (Proverbs 10:12; I Peter 4:8). God is love (I John 4:8). **Covering is the result of love—a protection and honor.**

**God doesn't cover the common things of this world.** He covers His treasures—like the Ark in the Holy Place. If we strolled along the sidewalks of Washington, D.C., we wouldn't happen across the Hope Diamond set out on a folding table. No. It's in the Smithsonian, not on the sidewalk. It's valuable. It's covered. It's protected.

## Holiness and Hair

What in the world do hair and holiness have to do with each other? Hair isn't holy and holiness isn't hair. Holy people, places, and things are not holy until they are dedicated to God. Holiness is about consecration, which means to be wholly committed to a specific purpose. Think of it this way. When you have an iPhone, you have to use their apps. Apple's not in the business of making apps for Blackberry users. They develop software functions set apart from those made for other phones because they are specifically designed to work with their own sweet techno-tools.

In the same way, holiness is set-apartness, or separation. It's not just separation *from* things (don't do this, don't do that), it's separated *for* things, like the phone apps we were talking about! And remember, you are the apple of His eye, and that's better than an Apple iPhone, an iPad, or a MacBook.

To be separated, we have to understand "lines of demarcation." What does that mean? We can't be separate without "lines" or boundaries. Girls, we don't get to set God's boundary lines. He set those in His Word.

"All scripture is given by inspiration of God, and is profitable for doctrine, for reproof, for correction, for instruction in righteousness" (II Timothy 3:16). Just look at that. Scripture sets the standard—that's doctrine, or God's commandments and directions taught to His people. His Word is given for reproof. That means we can prove ourselves against it, over and over again. It never changes; and when we use God's Word as our marking line, it corrects us when we're wrong. It tells us which side of the "line" we should be on—lines that separate God's people from nonbelievers. It instructs us on how to live the way we ought, ways acceptable to God.

Moses gives us a great example. God loved Moses. The Bible says there was no other prophet like him. Moses knew the Lord face to face. How cool would that be? Moses did miraculous signs and wonders in Egypt and in the desert. No one before or since has ever shown the mighty power or amazing things Moses performed before Pharaoh and Israel (Deuteronomy 34:10-12). The Bible tells us there has never been a more meek or humble man (Numbers 12:3). But in the record book, part of Moses' story, there's one little smudge. Just once he took matters into his own hands.

It may seem like a small thing. The Israelites were in the desert. They didn't have any water and they were worried. They turned to Moses, who turned to the Lord and asked what he should do. God told Moses to speak to a rock and water would come out of it. This wasn't the first time they faced a situation like this. When it happened previously, God told Moses to take his rod and hit a rock one time.

What happened in this second situation? Moses didn't follow the Lord's instructions. Instead of speaking to the rock, as God clearly instructed, Moses took his rod and hit the rock—not once, but twice. Water came, but so did judgment for Moses. This meek and humble man, the one God used to deliver the Israelites and set up the Tabernacle, was denied entry into the Promised Land. Why? God gives us the answer: "You did not uphold my holiness among the Israelites" (Deuteronomy 32:51, NIV). God was referring to this event with the rock, and after all Moses had done for Him, God didn't give him an opportunity to repent. Aren't we blessed that we still have the opportunity to get things right with God?

It seemed such an insignificant thing, but through this situation with Moses, God gives us a clear picture. **When we hear God's Word yet do things our own way, it does not uphold holiness.** If Moses suffered consequences,

Dear Abby,

I have oily scalp and dry ends. Do you have any advice that will help me deal with both the top and bottom of my hair?

Kathryn

Dear Kathryn,

There are lots of products on the market designed and packaged to deal with every hair condition. I did find a couple of treatments I could do with things I have at home that work great for me.

When I had an oily scalp, I put cider vinegar on it. I massaged it in until I got it all over my head and left it on for a few minutes. Then I rinsed it out with lukewarm water.

For the ends of my hair, I put a small amount of coconut oil on my hands and rub them together just enough to cover my hands. Then I rub the oil on the ends and work it about half way up my hair. Olive oil is good for this, too.

Abby

surely we will, too. We will miss out on blessings God has in store for us if we hear His Word and choose to do things our own way.

Holiness and hair. They are two different subjects, but related ones. How many rocks were out in the desert with Moses and the Israelites? I'm sure there were many, but God separated one out for a special purpose and expected Moses to honor and follow His instructions regarding it.

Holiness is more than just being filled with the Holy Spirit. It is a restoration of men and women to the condition they were in before sin. Don't forget that even in the garden paradise before sin entered, God still had some "off limits" boundaries—something that was separate just for Himself.

## Chapter Five

# Loose Ends

# Loose Ends

One thing I would like you to remember about the spirit of the world is that it is related to confusion and going after what you want. Paul spoke of that in Romans 7:21-23: "I find then a law, that when I would do good, evil is present with me. For I delight in the law of God after the inward man: but I see another law in my members, warring against the law of my mind." This conflict can cause frustration and resentment.

It's based on carnal senses and logic—like Eve allowing the serpent to twist God's instructions. When she listened to Satan, she made the wrong choice—to go for the power she thought she would get from knowledge. Prayer is the only way to convince the carnal nature to submit to the things which are good for the soul. A person who submits to God and is obedient to do those things that please Him will be open to His voice. His voice may be heard in various ways. Sometimes it may be audible, other times it may be "heard" only in the mind, and other times it comes through the pastor or the Sunday school teacher.

God responds to humility, not pride. God loves a cheerful giver, not a selfish taker. God says not to lean on our own understanding, but trust Him to give us direction for our paths. Satan whispers, "A path? Who needs it?"

It's easy to see when we put it in simple terms. Think about all the things God says love is in |I Corinthians 13.| Love is patient and kind. Love doesn't boast. It's not proud or self-seeking and isn't easily angered. Love doesn't keep a record of wrongs or delight in evil, but love rejoices in the truth!

A true Christian cannot conduct herself in impure ways. We are called to **purity**—to live free from things that contaminate or pollute. God is all about love and relationship. He's always there when we need to talk. He cares for our every need, but relationship with Him is not a "buffet" affair. We can't pick and choose with what we would like to fill our "God plates." **Relationship with God involves covenant.**

# Covenant

"Covenant" comes from the Latin word "convenire" which means "come together" or "convene." God wants to come together with us, His people, and He established an order so this could happen. You see, He is holy and we are not—but He loves us anyway. He wants to be in relationship with us. A Christian's first covenant must be with the Lord. Obedience to God is the way followers show their love for Him. Obedience is a basic requirement of all God's people (Isaiah 1:19; I Peter 1:14).

In the business world, most people are given responsibilities by their employer and usually do what is required of them. They have been asked to do certain things that they are capable of and most will find a way to do the job, even though it may seem difficult to carry out the request of the employer. This same principle applies in a believer's life. When we obey God's Word we can then be partakers of His promises.

"But the Lord is faithful, who shall stablish you, and keep you from evil. And we have confidence in the Lord touching you, that ye both do and will do the things which we command you. And the Lord direct your hearts into the love of God, and into the patient waiting for Christ" (II Thessalonians 3:3-5). **Covered by love—the love of God!**

Now, if you are still wondering about the mystery of those disappearing socks, it is a myth that dryers eat socks. They can't handle that much fiber in their diets. I read online the real answer: the combination of heat and the rotation of the dryer drum creates a vortex that allows the socks to be stolen by one-footed aliens from another galaxy. Just kidding! Remember, God called us to live upright, not uptight. It's OK to have some fun, even when we're talking about biblical principles.

# Is It Too Late?

Of course, people are going to mess up. God isn't looking for perfection—He's looking at our hearts. We're all gonna get "wet" now and then when we goof up and step outside our umbrellas in one way or another. When we get things wrong, we need to make them right, and that's that Tabernacle plan again we briefly touched on. Repentance is the first step, then an ordered approach to the presence of God in the secret place of the Most High.

> "Holy practice is the most decisive evidence
> of the reality of our repentance."
> —Jonathan Edwards

# God Wants Us to Have More!

I don't know about you, but I think God wants us to have so much more—and if that's what He wants, that's what I want. I believe it can happen, but it comes with a price. To have all God wants for our lives, we must give our all to Him.

I want to make sure you remember that the bride of Christ is not deprived, she is CHerisHed. She is protected. She is set apart for God. She is covered by LOVe.

91

If you recall, we touched very briefly on the story of "The Emperor's New Clothes"—a fairytale written by Hans Christian Anderson in 1837. The truth is, there's a real life story, and in it, it's not just the king walking around in his birthday suit. Every person, the entire human race is naked. I'm not talking about clothes on our outer bodies, but spiritually. Because of sin, we are all uncovered, unrighteous—naked before God. Every one of us has sinned and fallen short (Romans 3:23). Not one person has ever been perfect, and perfect is what the Law required us to be (James 2:10).

What hope do we have? A great and beautiful hope, but first we need to realize our condition. It's like the emperor when the little one shouted from the crowd what everyone knew but no one wanted to admit: "But he's not wearing anything at all!"

The truth is we need covering to stand before the Lord, and our hair, ladies, represents that to the world around us. People might look at us and wonder. They may think we're holding to some unnecessary tradition, but we know our hair is a picture of an uncut mystery—it's so much more than hair.

It would be a great tragedy to think we were properly covered, only to discover we were naked before the Lord. It doesn't matter how the tailors fluffed and preened about the emperor's clothes. It doesn't matter what people who don't know this precious truth believe or pressure us to believe. We must come before the Lord with the faith of a little child and admit our need for covering.

## But I Don't Wanna!

By now, you've worked through a lot of information. You've read every word. You even see covering in a different light, but you just "don't wanna." I've given you a lot to think about. I hope that you see the beauty and blessing we have to be God's "covered ones." We are His examples to those in this world, and in the spirit world, that we are His chosen, redeemed ones. It's an honor to be the example of Christ's covering for His church and God's divine order.

In addition to all the blessings to consider, the fact remains that Scripture doesn't speak in positive ways of women cutting their hair. Bible commentaries agree. *The New Schaff-Herzog Encyclopedia of Religious Knowledge* records, "Women never cut their hair." It also reads: "long hair was their greatest ornament," and to cut off a woman's hair "was the greatest … [humiliation]."[13] The Bible gives several verses on the shame associated with women cutting or losing their hair as judgment (Isaiah 3:24; Jeremiah 7:29; Ezekiel 7:18; I Corinthians 11:6). Documents have been uncovered that record the horrific treatment of women in Hitler's concentration camps. Among the many atrocities, women's hair was shaved and used to knit socks for the feet of their enemies.[14] This was a complete degradation of a woman's glory and crown.

Christians can settle for less than God wants us to have, but I hope you will choose to be like the Bereans who lived in Greece. This is what Luke said about them: "Now the Bereans were of more **noble character** than the Thessalonians, for they received the message with great eagerness and examined the Scriptures every day to see if what Paul said was true" (Acts 17:11, NIV).

God considered it of "more noble character" when the believers in this little city received Paul's teaching with eagerness and studied the Scriptures themselves. I would like to be in the group of people with "more noble character," wouldn't you? To do that, we have to open our hearts and study deeply in the Word to learn what God has to say.

When God reveals truth to us, we become responsible to that truth. We can't plead ignorance and say, "But I didn't know." We don't really have a choice anymore. We must walk in obedience to the revealed Word of God, and we can't fool God with clever hairdos.

"Apart from obedience, there can be no salvation, for salvation without obedience is a self-contradictory impossibility."
—A.W. Tozer

A person blessed to be in a church that teaches covering can't backpedal and expect God to bless them in spite of their choice to disregard His Word. That's like taking the lid, the Mercy Seat, off the Ark of the Covenant. If God's people even touched the Ark inappropriately, there was judgment (II Samuel 6:6-7). The Philistines, Israel's enemies, actually lifted the Ark's covering and put in offerings of golden figures. They got off without any consequences after the Ark was sent off on a cart (I Samuel 6:4). When the Ark drifted into Israelite land, over fifty thousand people died when they dared to take off its covering and look inside (I Samuel 6:19). The Philistines weren't judged the same way God's people were judged. **God's people have to do things God's way.** God's blessings come with responsibilities.

Later King David tried moving the Ark with a cart. It worked for the Philistines, but again God's people suffered the penalty. They had wandered away from the Scriptures and forgotten the Ark must be carried on poles by priests. They had lost their understanding of how to interact with the Ark and the glory of God. When God's people wander from God's ways, they face harsh consequences.

It's a dangerous thing to know something and not do it. It brings into question the sincerity of a person who calls herself a committed follower of God and reeks of immaturity's dirty diapers. A person seeking God with all her heart, soul, mind, and

> DON'T LEARN FROM YOUR OWN MISTAKES—
>
> LEARN FROM THE MISTAKES OF OTHERS.

strength doesn't ask, "Do I have to?" when she sees the truth in the Word. We get to! I have found in my life that I never regret obeying God—but I always regret ignoring what He asks me to do.

Remember that God's guidelines are because He wants to be in an interactive relationship. "I will be a Father to you, and you shall be My sons and daughters, says the LORD Almighty. Therefore, having these promises, beloved, let us cleanse ourselves from all filthiness of the flesh and spirit, perfecting holiness in the fear of God" (II Corinthians 6:18-7:1, NKJV).

Once you see the beauty in God's covering, I hope you won't allow the pull of others to influence your decision to honor God with this small sacrifice. It's only natural to want to feel accepted by others, but sometimes we have to draw some lines. We simply must choose Jesus over the things of the world (I John 2:15). Why would we miss out on the blessings of God to fit in with people who don't love Him or value the things we hold dear? We shouldn't be embarrassed or ashamed to be different if we're being different for Jesus. Remember, Jesus' words: "Whosoever therefore shall be ashamed of me and of my words in this adulterous and sinful generation; of him also shall the Son of man be ashamed, when he cometh in the glory of his Father with the holy angels" (Mark 8:38).

Because Jesus has been so good, sacrificing His life for us, He has the right to ask each of us to present our bodies "a living sacrifice, holy, acceptable unto God." This is our "reasonable service." He calls us to be separate, to not conform to this world, but be "transformed by the renewing of your

mind, that ye may prove what is that good, and acceptable, and perfect, will of God" (Romans 12:1-2). In other words, we do what we do because we belong to Him, not in order to belong to Him. We follow His ways because we love Him, not as a requirement to earn His love.

A life of obedience to God and His Word serves as the believers' witness to others and is a compliment to their testimony. Christ is our Savior, and no true Christian should ever be ashamed to obey His Word.

It's not a light thing for a person to reject God's Word once he has received it. If you've read this entire book and still haven't chosen to let your hair grow, I hope you will carefully and prayerfully study the Word of God on your own. Perhaps God will open your understanding as you read, or through the teaching of others. If you are in a church where your leadership asks the church to abide by this teaching, I counsel you to "have confidence in your leaders and submit to their authority, because they keep watch over you as those who must give an account. Do this so that their work will be a joy, not a burden, for that would be of no benefit to you" (Hebrews 13:17, NIV).

# Delight God . . . Delight in God

Having uncut hair doesn't make a person a Christian any more than wearing an apron makes them a chef. When someone loves God and reverences His

DeLiGHt iN God

Word, she should be continually growing and learning and putting into practice the biblical principles she learns.

"I delight to do thy will, O my God: yea, thy law is within my heart" (Psalm 40:8). When we walk in His will, we walk in agreement with His purposes and His plans. That's an awesome way to live, because God's plans are for our good (Jeremiah 29:11).

If our desire is to please someone, we wouldn't give them what *we* want them to have, but what we know *they* want. Did you ever get a present like that? Say your friend Sally is big into zebra prints, but you are a camo girl, and Sally knows it. For Christmas Sally buys you a huge zebra-print purse with a matching cell phone case. That was a gift that would have made her happy, not you, and you're supposed to smile, be thankful, and use it at holiday youth convention. Awkward.

The Bible is like God's "Christmas catalog." It has His "wish list" of sorts—everything in it He likes. He told us what He wants, and giving Him what He wants shows respect for who He is. When we give Him what He asks of us, He comes back with so much more (II Kings 3:16-18). The Bible says when we delight ourselves in Him, He will give us the desires of our hearts (Psalm 37:4). Those are the deep things we long for in the inner core of who we are.

"Keep therefore the words of this covenant, and do them, that ye may prosper in all that ye do" (Deuteronomy 29:9). When we obey, we not only delight God, but we bless ourselves—in *all* we do! There's a splashover effect! I obey God in one area; His blessings are so big they splash over into others. It's like Shamu the whale soaking the first two rows of spectators at Sea World. If you're there, you're bound to get wet!

Did you know that even children are blessed by their parents' obedience (Deuteronomy 28:4)? There are blessings when we walk with God in His paths, but I must give you a word of caution. It's not safe when a person hears the words of the covenant and receives the blessing and then persists in going her own way. That person thinks she's safe, but her decision will bring disaster (Deuteronomy 29:19).

Call me a blessing chaser! I'm after God and everything He wants me to have. I believe there is a great, positive reward for doing things God's ways. I don't want to focus on the negative but do feel to share three verses of Scripture as we conclude to help any who may still be struggling with "don't wannas."

*"Woe to the rebellious children, saith the LORD, that take counsel, but not of me; and that cover with a covering, but not of my spirit, that they may add sin to sin" (Isaiah 30:1).*

*"We lie down in our shame, and our confusion covereth us: for we have sinned against the LORD our God, we and our fathers, from our youth even unto this day, and have not obeyed the voice of the LORD our God" (Jeremiah 3:25).*

*"Thus saith the LORD, Stand ye in the ways, and see, and ask for the old paths, where is the good way, and walk therein, and ye shall find rest for your souls. But they said, We will not walk therein" (Jeremiah 6:16).*

Remember, the old paths aren't good because they are old but because they are tried and proven. Try them. Prove Him. Be blessed. Be a blessing. Be covered by His love.

Dear Abby,

What do you say when people tell you your hair would look healthier if you got it trimmed?

Tiffany

Dear Tiffany,

Most people tell me my hair is pretty, but sometimes I get questions like this, too. First, I have to remember that my hair is much more than a toenail that needs clipping because it gets too long. My hair is more than a physical thing on my head. It really does have a connection to who I am spiritually. So for the people who don't understand this, it's usually best to take a non-defensive, light approach.

I believe the Bible teaches that I am blessed and that I please God when I allow my hair to grow to the length He has chosen for me. In my opinion, trimming has nothing to do with keeping my hair healthy. Keeping my hair healthy is keeping it clean, using good shampoo and conditioner, and trying not to burn it with a straightener or curling iron. Taking care of hair at the scalp, where it grows, and not over-processing it with styling tools or treatments, are the best ways to maintain good hair health.

Abby

## Chapter Six

# "Hairticulture"

# "Hairticulture"

A thread of hair is made up of strands of protein called keratin. The only living part is the piece still inside the scalp in a little pocket called a follicle where cells bunch together to create a strand. Attached to every follicle are both a small muscle and an oil gland. Oil from the gland keeps the hair soft, and that little muscle is what gives us goose bumps. When a person is afraid or cold, the muscle contracts and causes hair to stand up.

Most people have around one hundred thousand hairs on their heads, with a range anywhere from eighty thousand up to one hundred fifty thousand. Who generally have the most? The answer surprised me. Blonds generally have the most hair per head, while redheads have the least.

Mary, Mary, quite contrary, how does your hair shaft grow? Well, I'm sure you're not contrary like the girl in the nursery rhyme of old, but you've probably wondered just how hair grows. No, there are no silver bells and cockle shells, but things do come together, little cells, in orderly lines that grow like pretty maids all in a row.

An individual soft thread of hair, also called a shaft, grows for two to six years then rests for about three months. When naptime is over, the hair begins to grow again, and a new hair pushes the old one out at the root. That's why most people lose fifty to one hundred hairs every day. It's a natural process, a growth/loss/re-growth cycle that happens continually throughout our lifetimes.

That means the hair you have today is not the same hair you had six years ago, and it will be completely replaced in the next six years, as well.

Hair grows about an inch a month—more quickly in the summer months than in the winter. When uncut, hair normally grows to a length of two to three feet. Most hair has a sort of programming built in that predetermines the length it will grow until it falls out in its natural (God-given) conclusion. Just like your eye color, your height, and other physical features, God has determined the length your hair is able to grow. Some people think cutting hair causes it to grow faster, but according to Ruth Freeman Swain, author of *Hairdo: What We Do and Did to Our Hair*,[15] "Seasons, age, diet, and health affect hair growth: cutting hair does not."

## Healthy Hair

For healthy hair, you have to start with a healthy you, and that starts with eating healthy foods. In particular, cheese, lean protein, eggs, fish, and nuts help your hair grow strong, while milk, fruits, and veggies keep it healthy. It's also important to drink lots of water and get enough sleep.

103

Hair is affected by diet, stress, illness, medicines, wind, sun, salt, hormonal changes, and severe heat/cold. Especially if your hair is dry or damaged, it is a good idea to use hair products that contain sunscreen and wear a hat in extreme temperatures.

## Q&A

Dear Gabby,

Some people tell me women of color should cut their hair to keep it from breaking. What do you think?

Nadia

Dear Nadia,

I've never cut my hair so I can't give an answer based on personal experience, but I find that if I use the right products for my hair, I don't have problems with breakage. The key is not letting my hair get too dry.

For me, I choose not to cut my hair. Nobody makes me. I just choose to because God instructed me to. It's in the Bible. I may not completely understand why, but I want to be obedient. So I let my hair grow to its natural length.

I have a friend who used to cut her hair. She says that her hair grew when she cut it, but not as much as it does now. She hasn't cut her hair for twelve years, and she doesn't have a problem with breakage as long as she keeps her hair and scalp healthy and properly moisturized. She also recommends braiding to keep down breakage.

Gabby

Dear Gabby,

Do you ever feel different when you are around girls who have long hair knowing your hair can't grow very long?

Shaniqua

Dear Shaniqua,

God made me who I am, and that includes my hair. I do feel different sometimes, but I just don't see the point in trying to wish for something I can't have. I try to be thankful instead for what I do have.

Whenever I feel bothered, I pray about it. I pray God will help me accept me for who I am. I also pray my hair grows, and I remind myself this is how God made me.

Gabby

Dear Abby,

My neighbor got gum stuck in her hair and her mom cut it out. She said she didn't know how else to deal with it. Is there any way to get gum out of hair without cutting it?

Heather

Dear Heather,

Here's a simple, scissor-free way to get gum out of your hair. Just rub ice on it until the gum hardens then you can get the gum out without cutting your hair. I've heard peanut butter works, too.

Abby

Out of the Blue

Answering the phone one day at work, I heard the voice of a young man looking for a church like the one his grandmother had attended. As a young child, he often spent summers with his grandma, and she took him to church. He remembered what he felt, but he didn't know the name of the church. That's why he was calling. He was on a search.

He explained that his grandma was the only one in her family who attended this church. Others in the family made fun of her beliefs and her lifestyle that was very different from theirs. "They just didn't understand," he told me with feeling. "She didn't live that way because she *had* to, but because she *wanted* to." Even as a child he recognized the difference between loving devotion to God and just following rules. Grandma lived the way she did because of her pure love for the Lord.

—Mary Loudermilk

## Hair: It's Personal and Individual

Your hair is a major identifying factor. Is it thick or fine? Curly or straight? What color? All these attributes create a picture of you.

Have you ever wondered what determines a person's hair color? Natural hair colors are the result of one of two pigments produced inside hair follicles. Pigments are substances that produce color, and for hair, one pigment creates dark-blond, brown, and black, and another results in red. Blond hair occurs when there is not enough pigment in the strand to create color. Grey hair happens when pigment decreases or disappears altogether.

Regardless of the mane you're sporting on your head, the main thing is learning to work with what you've been given. Not every style works or holds with every type of hair. We'll go over some tips and tricks to help you increase your options and make your hair look its very best.

There are four basic hair types: straight, wavy, kinky, and curly; and three subcategories: thick, medium, and fine. Any of these can also be subdivided into normal, oily, or dry determined by the amount of oil produced by the oil gland in the follicles. Busy glands make oily hair. Not-so-busy glands leave you with dry hair. Lastly, hair can range from slippery smooth to hay-bale coarse.

If you have straight hair, you know it can sometimes be more difficult to work with because it has a tendency to slip and fall out of hairdos. It's often hard to curl and shape, especially when it is very fine. Be careful to avoid over-processing fine and straight hair in an effort to make it do things it just wasn't meant to do. Instead, make the most of its natural advantage. Straight hair is generally shinier than other types. Play it up with a sleek style.

When working with fine hair that is slipping out of your hairdos, try using a thickener or spray to add a bit of texture and make your hair more manageable.

Wavy hair is the least common type of hair. It is more pliable and generally thicker than other hair types. Wavy hair holds curls well and can also be straightened, so you have more styling options.

Curly hair is pretty but can sometimes be high maintenance. It is often coarse in texture, and that can make hair look dry. It's important to keep curly hair moisturized and avoid over-processing that can cause it to be frizzy. The advantage to curly hair is that it gives you a lot of versatility when it comes to styling—from simple ponytails to more complicated up-dos. Curly hair can also be straightened, and because it comes out of the head with a natural lift, it can be easily shaped into a variety of styles.

Kinky hair can come in a number of textures from fine to thick and is generally the most delicate hair type. Any chemical or heat treatments should be used with caution to avoid breakage. But even with its weaknesses, this hair type has some great advantages. It has a beautiful sheen and can be fashioned into styles both sleek and curly that other hair types can't support.

When blowing out kinky hair, begin with a wide-tooth comb that works more easily through your hair, and then switch to a fine-tooth comb for finishing.

# Washing

Dirt sticks to the oil that coats our hair, and salty sweat makes hair dirty, too. For routine maintenance, hair should be washed a minimum of once or twice a week. You do not need to wash your hair every day. This can cause your scalp to dry out. Do, however, always wash out chlorine.

Our scalps make natural oils, some more than others. When choosing a shampoo, select one suited to your hair type. Regardless of what the bottle says, most people only need to apply shampoo once, not rinse and repeat, unless their hair is especially dirty. If your hair fits more than one category, you can try switching up shampoos and conditioners each time you wash. Concentrate on the scalp one washing and the ends another.

When you wash your hair, it cleans and opens the outer layer of the hair shaft so it readily absorbs conditioners and other products. Before and after conditioning, make sure you rinse well or your hair will feel sticky and get dirty more quickly.

If your hair is dry on the ends but limp at the roots, put conditioner on the length of your hair before you shampoo. This will protect it from being dried further by the shampoo. When you wash, focus your scrubbing at the scalp without working the shampoo into the longer hair. The bubbles running off as you rinse will sufficiently clean the rest of your hair.

Occasional use of a clarifying shampoo can get rid of product buildup, mineral buildup from hard water, and salt buildup from water softeners. Keep in mind that the more product you use, the more buildup you will have. That may affect how often you use a clarifying shampoo. Getting rid of buildup will increase your hair's shine.

To deep-clean your scalp, stimulate it with a little plastic scrubber, but don't overdo. **Remember that your scalp is just skin with hair attached. Don't treat it any more harshly than you would the skin on the rest of your body.**

Different shampoos do different jobs. Body-building shampoos clean hair without conditioners that smooth down the hair. This makes your hair feel fuller. Volumizing shampoos, usually made with panthenol or vitamin B-5, can "pump up" the hair making it look fuller.

Special shampoos are also available for oily hair. Tea shampoos have an astringent effect that can remove excess oil from your hair. If you're dealing with oily hair, you may want to skip the daily rinse-out conditioners, or just apply them to the ends of your hair. You may also try applying shampoo to your hair while it is dry, before working in water.

Have you ever been desperate to wash your hair but there was no way you could get the job done? Beauty supplies carry no-rinse and dry shampoos that can see you through emergency situations such as no access to water or being bedridden due to illness. Dry shampoos are sprayed directly onto hair and penetrate the hair absorbing dirt and hair products. All the impurities are simply brushed out, and you are left with clean, soft hair. No-rinse shampoos can be lathered in to dry hair and towel dried.

While we're talking about washing, remember to wash your brushes and combs in warm soapy water.

Dear Gabby,

A hairdresser told me not to comb my hair when it's wet, but when I comb it when it's dry, I have a harder time getting the comb through. I end up losing more hair and having more breakage. What do you do?

Letha

Dear Letha,

I know some hairdressers tell you not to comb through wet hair, but I've had the same experience you have. This is what I do. After I wash my hair, I put conditioner in it, and while I'm still in the shower, I comb it as gently as possible. This distributes the conditioner and I can work the comb through more easily than when it's dry. Then, after I get out of the shower, it's much easier to comb through my hair before styling.

Gabby

# Conditioners

Conditioners trap moisture in your hair making it softer and easier to manage. Just be careful not to make it too soft or you'll have to add excessive amounts of gels and sprays to style it. Adjust the weight of the conditioner to the weight and thickness of your hair. For example, for fine hair, use a product that won't soften your hair. Normal hair may only need conditioner on the ends, and thick hair can benefit from conditioners that smooth hair and decrease volume. It's possible to over-condition your hair. If that happens, wash your hair with a clarifying shampoo.

Even though some shampoos have conditioners in them, often long hair benefits from the extra conditioning treatment of a separate product. One good way to distribute conditioner through your hair is with a wide-tooth comb. Gently combing the conditioner through can also make your rinsing more effective and your hair less tangled. Overall, conditioners are great for your hair, but the soothing and softening ingredients (emollients) can also weigh your hair down. Be careful not to use too much, especially if your hair tends to be limp.

Special reconstructing conditioners can help keep your long hair healthy and prevent it from getting too dry. You may not need to use one every time, but a reconstructing conditioner can rebuild and improve dry or damaged hair by adding moisture and nutrients.

If you deal with static or frizzy hair, this is very often the result of dryness. Try a leave-in conditioner.

Protein treatments can repair damaged, weakened hair, but don't use them too often. They can dry out your hair. If your hair needs repair, use a protein treatment once a week for a month, then switch to once or a twice a month.

# Tangles

It's amazing how different hair types vary so drastically in how much they do or do not tangle. Some girls comb right through their hair with very little effort, while others require more time and attention. One thing you can do to minimize after-shampooing tangles is to brush your hair out thoroughly before washing. If you wake up with a nesty tangle in the morning, brush your hair out at night and sleep in a single braid. It's comfy, and you'll wake up tangle-free.

For those who need some extra help in the tangle department, silicone-based products can be used in place of or in addition to conditioners. To use, you just rub a drop in the palms of your hands and smooth into wet hair.

A cream rinse can also be helpful in detangling. Just keep in mind that detanglers don't replace conditioners. They do different jobs, and make sure to rinse products out well to avoid leaving residue on your hair that can make it limp or look dull.

Another way to cut down on after-shampooing tangles is with a simple washing technique. Make sure you start with untangled hair, and while it is hanging straight, put some shampoo at the top. Work the lather down the length of your hair with a gentle zigzag motion. To clean the scalp, use small circular motions with the pads of your fingers so you don't ball up your hair while you're washing it.

 When brushing or combing out tangles, hold the hair above the tangle to keep it from pulling and hurting your head.

Pat wet hair with a towel instead of attempting to rub the water out of it. Air-drying is best for overall hair health, but if you use a blow dryer, hold it away from your head. Avoid drying your hair in every direction which increases tangles. Tangles are more than just a pain in the neck, and if you've ever had your head yanked by someone pulling one out, you know what I mean. Avoiding tangles as much as possible is good because fewer tangles mean fewer breakages and split ends.

Dear Abby,

Why is it wrong to just trim my hair? Isn't that different than cutting? Just wondering.

Mandy

Dear Mandy,

How could you go about trimming your hair without cutting it? You would do it the same way, whether you call it cutting or trimming. What if a new convert has really short hair—would she have the same right to keep her hair trimmed? I would think so, and then where would be the distinction? I Corinthians 11:15 says this: "But if a woman have long hair, it is a glory to her: for her hair is given her for a covering." Would you really want your covering to be inadequate to stand before God or to be an example of His love?

Abby

# Split Ends

Conditioners, which we've already discussed, do help with split ends. They "close down" the outer part of the hair to make it smoother. After you wash your hair, use a rinse-out conditioner or a leave-in conditioner in the ends. To avoid breakage, it's best to use a wide-toothed comb on dry hair. Wet hair is more fragile than dry hair.

If you're able, deep condition your hair once a month. For the best results, use a pre-wash deep conditioner. Work the product of your choice in from the root to the tip of your hair and then cover your head with a plastic cap, tucking all the hair inside. Wrap the cap in a hot, damp towel and leave it on for ten to thirty minutes. If you have access to a bonnet-type hair dryer, sitting under one can really open up hair to receive the moisturizing benefits of deep conditioning treatments. A warm towel will work in the same way to open the outer (cuticle) layer of the hair. Rinse your hair with the coldest water you can stand to lock in the moisture. This treatment will increase your hair's shine, health, and strength and help close up split ends. Even if you don't have a special deep conditioner, using this process with your everyday conditioner once a week can really make a difference.

For an easy overnight treatment without buying a special deep conditioner, work a generous amount of thick hand cream (not lotion) into your hair. Braid it or put it in a bun overnight, then wash it out in the morning. Your hair will be softer and shinier.

|To minimize split ends, avoid overuse of hot styling tools like blow dryers and curling irons.| If you use curling irons or straighteners, make sure your hair is completely dry. Hair serums can help prevent breakage, and there are specially designed products for use with hot styling tools.

Along with the "anti-breakage" shampoos and conditioners available in the marketplace, here's a home remedy to try:

Mash up an avocado and apply to your hair while it is damp. Leave it on for twenty minutes then wash and condition as normal. For an extra boost, add some hot olive oil into the mashed avocado and while it is still warm, gently work the mixture into your hair. Cover it with a plastic cap or warm towel. Rinse in cold water.

Gail Duff, author of *Natural Beauty*[16], offers another simple treatment you can try. It is made of two ingredients you probably already have at home. Put two tablespoons of clear honey in a bowl and beat in one-third cup of warm olive oil. Massage it into your hair, wrap your hair in a hot towel, and leave it for thirty minutes. Rinse with warm water. She recommends using an egg shampoo followed by a rinse of warm water with one tablespoon of cider vinegar.

And yet one more split-ends remedy. It's a bit more time consuming, and not something you'd do every day, but I thought I'd include it if you'd like to give it a try for a special occasion.

- Shampoo your hair with a moisturizing formula.
- Use a good rinse-out conditioner, focusing some extra attention on the ends.
- Rinse well with cold water and blot out extra moisture with a towel.
- Apply a leave-in conditioner and detangle with a wide-toothed comb.
- Rub a small drop of shine serum in the palms of your hands and then run your hands over your hair, again with a focus on the ends.

- Dry your hair completely using a large paddle brush, smoothing hair as you dry it to make the ends as straight as possible.
- After your hair is completely dry, spray on a light layer of heat protectant product then use a heated straightener on the ends of your hair. Finish with a light spray of hair spray.

If you don't have the time or inclination to try this treatment, you may opt to use a bit of silicone-based "shiner" on split ends. These close the cuticle down and give a smoother look to your hair. Shiner can be used on the full length of your hair as well and is best applied to dry or only slightly damp hair.

**Your scalp and hair can benefit from regular oil massages, especially if you have dry skin.** Apply a lukewarm oil like coconut, olive, or almond and gently massage it into your hair before washing. This is particularly beneficial if you have an itchy scalp, and peppermint oil can be especially soothing.

Different shampoos give more or less lather. The amount of suds doesn't equal the amount of cleaning. Some shampoos create very little lather, and with most shampoos, the dirtier your hair, the less suds you will see.

What's a *cowlick*? Well, it's not something you really get from a sloppy bovine encounter, although the name does originate from what happens to a calf after her mama licks her over and over. A cowlick is a section of hair that stands straight up or lies at an angle that's different from the rest of your hair. They happen when hair grows in a spiral in one section, usually on the crown, but they can show up anywhere.

If you've locked horns with a cowlick, here's a tip to end your tussle and get that wayward hair going in the right direction. Using a blow dryer and brush, focus some warm air at the root while you brush the hair back and forth. Once the hair is no longer bucking every which way but loose, blow a stream of cool air on it to set it in place.

# Dandruff

Dandruff is caused when the skin on your scalp becomes dry and flakes into tiny pieces of dead skin. It can happen for several reasons, and it's important to know the cause before you choose a treatment.

If you suffer from severe dandruff, use medicated shampoos and oils, following the directions on the packages.

Oily dandruff comes from an oily scalp and shampoos have been developed that have some extra umph in the scrub department. They have some abrasiveness that can clean excess oil from the scalp. Shampoos designed to treat dry dandruff add moisturizers to your hair.

Keep in mind these shampoos, for oily or dry dandruffs, work only for non-medical conditions. You may need to see a doctor or dermatologist if eczema or psoriasis is causing your scalp to flake.

Regardless of the shampoo and remedy, make sure to rinse your hair well after washing and treatments. Everyone should rinse their hair for at least sixty to ninety seconds. If you have dry hair, rinse in warm water. If you have oily hair, rinse in cool water. When you're finished, your hair should feel clean, without any trace of coatings on it. You may think you have dandruff, when actually you are just not getting all the product rinsed from your hair. Gel, especially, can flake and look like dandruff.

One natural remedy for dandruff is to rub a lime on your scalp. Let the juice sit for ten minutes and then wash normally.

## Hair Styles

"Really good hair acts like the frame on a beautiful painting, not overwhelming or upstaging the artistry it surrounds."[17]

When we talked about modesty in *The Girl in the Dress*, one of the topics we discussed was being moderate and appropriate. These are principles that apply to our hairdos as well. We want to be a witness, not something the world gawks at. That includes the way we style our hair and the things we use in our hair as well, such as flowers, bows, feathers—all types of adornment.

# Styling Tips

For best results when you're fixing your hair, you first need to know its natural texture and what products and techniques to use for different styles.

Only use products where you need them. If you are looking for some extra lift at the roots, just apply product on your scalp. If you're only curling the ends, use styling product on the ends. This will not only help you avoid buildup, but can also save some money on products like gels, mousses, and sprays.

Want more lift at your part? Spray just the part area with a spray styling gel or special root-lifting product.

# Styling Products

There are so many different hair products out there, how in the world can we know which ones are right for our hair? Here are three pointers:

1. Gels are great for both defining curls and waves—also for straightening hair.
2. Sprays can be used for adding volume and body.
3. Grooming products smooth hair and decrease volume.

## Word on the Street

Walking across the parking lot one day while I was shopping, I ran into a lady just getting out of her car. She looked at me, noticed my long hair, and got really excited. After complimenting my hair, she asked, "Do you know that the Bible teaches a woman should have long hair? I'm letting mine grow, and I can hardly wait until it gets long!"

She was bubbling with joy that God had shown her this truth in His Word. Her understanding seemed to come from her personal study of God's Word and His revealed truth rather than from what someone else had told her.

—Mary Loudermilk

Many hairdressers recommend using a protective thermal styling spray or silicone whenever you are going to use a heated appliance on your hair. Not only will they protect your hair from damage from the heat, but they also keep curling irons and curlers from getting caught in your hair.

For fine hair, use mousse to give fullness and lift. Gels can also be used, applied at the root. **Clear gels leave you with the best shine.** If the gel you bought seems too thick, add a bit of water before you apply it to your hair. This can reduce stiffness.

A word of caution. If you're using a lot of product in your hair, be careful when you comb or brush it out. Forcing combs and brushes through your hair can cause it to break and split. If you have an unusually heavy amount of product in your hair and you are afraid to brush it before washing, try using a hot rinse before you wash. This will dissolve some of the product out before following your normal hair care routine.

# Blow Dryers

For optimal hair health, it's best not to use a blow dryer every time you wash your hair, but when you need one, here are some considerations:

- Select one that is a comfortable weight and size for your hand.
- Make sure the fan has a cover over it so you don't get your hair sucked in.
- Professionals recommend at least 1,200 watts, but up to 2,000, with multiple heat settings.
- If you have to dry curly hair and you don't want to lose the curl, try a diffuser. These are optional attachments for blow dryers that can soften the flow of air and protect your curls. They can also be used if you've set your hair on regular curlers and want to heat up the hair a bit to hold the curl.
- That nozzly thing on the end of your blow dryer is there for a reason. You can use it to focus the air on one section at a time. If you blow your hair all over the place, the result is more tangles and flyaways.

- To keep your blow dryer blowing, clean the screens on its backside. Sometimes these are detachable, but if not, just use a damp cloth and wipe them down.
- Remember not to over-dry your hair, and be careful about the combs and brushes you use when drying. Plastic can melt, so pick a sturdy comb or brush, preferably made of hard rubber. For drying long hair, a large blow-drying brush works well—or a vented brush made especially for blow drying.
- When you're drying your hair with a dryer, there are different techniques for different results. To add volume, use a round brush underneath the hair you are drying and twirl it down the length of your hair as you dry it. To straighten curls or smooth hair, brush or comb from the top. One technique that will give you smooth hair and reduce volume is to comb down the hair with warm air trailing directly behind the comb. Follow this with a second combing and a stream of cool air. Regardless of the technique, keep your comb or brush moving through your hair to prevent over-drying and avoid making bumps or lines.
- When you are using a blow dryer to remove moisture, keep the appliance eight to ten inches away from your hair. When using a lower setting for styling, keep it four to six inches away.

Heat makes volume, while cool air smoothes your hair.

## Curling and Flat Irons

Curling irons vary in size from tiny to very wide. Pick the size barrel for the size of curl you like. You may decide to purchase more than one size to create different looks. Look for one that offers you more than one heat setting and is easy for you to use. Curling irons come in a variety of coatings, from chrome to gold, ceramic to velvet, and even Teflon (that non-stick surface on your frying pan). The ones least damaging are made of ceramic.

Flat irons are used for flattening hair (no brainer). In addition to straightening and smoothing, they can also be used to crimp or wave with detachable plates.

It's best to use hot tools on dry hair, and remember to clean any styling iron you use on your hair. Stylist Kevin Mancuso[17] recommends spraying and wiping your irons down with oven cleaner. He also recommends keeping a spray bottle filled with water near to spray on the irons for a quick cool down if they are too hot.

When using a curling iron, start with the hair closest to your head. Begin by opening the clamp and winding your hair around the barrel, but leaving the ends sticking out. Lightly pump the clamp so the hair moves around the curling iron and catches in the ends. This will keep you from ironing in lines or having uncurled ends. After the iron is in just a few seconds, release your hair by opening the clamp and pulling the hair out sideways, not down. If you have hard-to-curl hair, try putting the curl in a non-heated roller for a few minutes immediately after removing it from the curling iron. When the hair is cool, take the curler out, and you should have a longer-lasting curl.

## Curlers

Hot curlers have the same qualities as curling irons and are also made of many similar materials. Use the same guidelines to |choose the curlers right for you.|

When using curlers of any type, make sure you roll your hair in the direction you want the curl, and when you are unwinding, don't pull the curler down. This can cause the hair to get caught. Carefully unroll hair by unwinding it at your side.

In addition to hot rollers that use heat to add curl or waves to your hair, you also have other curling options. Steam rollers give moist heat and work well for people with dry hair. Sponge rollers are a good choice for delicate hair. They make the best curls when your hair is damp (with water or styling product) and wound tightly on the curler. Sponge rollers give a great, long-lasting curl. Bendable stick rollers are also gentler on hair than heated ones. Self-sticking spike rollers are not good to use with long hair. Hair gets snagged in the spikes and tangles easily.

If you like curls, but don't want to use heat or rollers, pin curls are an option you might want to consider. These can be made by twisting sections of hair gently from the ends to the root. **The tightness of the twist will affect the tightness of the curl.** With the fingers of one hand close to your head, wind the twisted hair around them with the other. Slide the curl off your fingers onto your head and secure in place with two bobby pins crossed into an "x." Wrap your hair with a scarf if you will be sleeping on pin curls.

Finger curls and loops are another option that require no heat, appliances, or curlers. They are similar to pin curls, but are not twisted. Simply roll sections of hair around your fingers or make loops. Secure in the same manner as the pin curls. These can be removed and styled, or left in place for an elegant up-do.

# Brushing and Combing

I've heard of ladies who devoutly brush their hair one hundred strokes every night. Brushing hair with a good brush is good for your scalp. It stimulates the blood flow and spreads oil from your hair follicles throughout your hair which helps keep it soft. It also loosens buildup around follicles, clearing away dead cells, dust, and dirt. Yes, daily brushing is good, but be careful not to yank excessively.

Some people are afraid to brush because they think it makes their hair fall out. Brushing your hair when it is dry does not cause you to lose hair. It actually removes the hair that is already loose because of the natural growth cycle. However, brushing your hair vigorously when it is wet can lead to hair loss and increased split ends.

To pick the right brush for you, you first need to know your hair type. The thicker the hair, the less dense and more rigid the bristles of your brush should be. For fine hair, use a brush with lots of soft bristles. Brushes with metal bristles should only be used if their tips have little balls on the ends and the base of the brush is flexible. Paddle brushes are best for brushing out long hair.

Well, we've talked about cows, let's talk about a member of the pig family. I know it sounds bizarre, but the best brushes are made out of boar bristles. Yes, I really mean brushes made out of short, stiff hog hairs. Oink! If you think brushing your hair with boar bristles is gross, consider that toothbrushes used to be made from the same stubble. Gross and double oink!

What's so special about boar bristle brushes? They are gentler on your hair than other brushes and distribute the natural oils from the scalp all the way to the ends of your hair. That can boost your hair's shine factor. One word of advice before you run out to buy one. Some people, usually those with thick hair, find the boar bristle brushes don't have the stiffness they need to get through their hair. If that's the case for you (it is for me), brushes are available that are made with a mix of nylon and natural bristles.

If you need to brush out waves or curls, do it from underneath. You probably don't want to brush out your curls altogether unless you are planning to straighten them or pull them into a sleeker hairstyle.

# Combs

Choose the right comb for the job. Fine- to medium-tooth combs are best for backcombing and detangling. Wide-tooth combs work well for distributing conditioner through your hair. Tailed combs are great for parting hair, and wide combs or picks give some lift to waves and curls.

# Elastics and Pins

To prevent your hair from breaking and getting caught in your ponytails, use holders or elastics that are covered in fabric. Rubber-tipped bobby pins are gentler on your scalp.

# Rats

If you have difficulty getting your hair up, especially because it's fine, thin, or slippery, you might try a foundational support known, believe it or not, as a rat. What is with all the animals in this hair-care chapter? I don't know, but I do know a rat can help you get your hair up and keep it up.

## Getting a Little Lift

Speaking of rats, what your mom probably called "ratting" or "teasing" is today known by a more accurate term: |"back combing."| This technique gives your hair some lift off the scalp.

Back combing can be done to your entire head or to spots where you want more fullness. To begin, take a small section of hair and brush it smooth. From the back side of the hair, use a fine-toothed comb or brush to comb backwards several times—down the hair just above the root line. You may want to only do a bit close to your crown, or go higher up the length of your hair for more fullness and support for your hairdo. Just make sure you aren't pulling your hair too tightly. Hold it loosely as you back comb and then lightly brush the top layer to smooth out the look.

# Zigzag

If you like the fun look of a zigzaggy part, here's how to do it. Grab your tailed comb and use the tip to swivel a quick squiggly line. Make sure to keep the comb touching your head from the beginning to the end of the part.

## Tucked Ends

If you have a ponytail and you would like to make a loop, first fasten the end of your hair together with a bobby pin then secure it under your ponytail with a couple of criss-crossed pins.

## Headache Helper

The next time you get a headache, try this little remedy. Take a section of hair about one inch from the scalp and gently pull it for a few seconds. Work your way around your head. This can increase circulation and reduce painful headaches.

# Real Beauty

Everyone wants to be beautiful. That's a normal, universal desire that continually feeds billions of dollars into the beauty industry. But consider this wonderful beautifier that won't lighten your wallet one penny: **"For the LORD taketh pleasure in his people: he will beautify the meek with salvation" (Psalm 149:4).**

When the Holy Ghost is resident and active in our lives, God gives us a supernatural injection that beautifies us like nothing else. Nope. Not botox. I'm talking about salvation. Salvation beauty treatments—offered free of charge every day!

# Endnotes

1. A.A. Milne, *The House at Pooh Corner* (New York, NY: Dutton Children's Books, 1928).

2. *http://www.dictionary.com*

3. *http://www.ctlibrary.com/ch/1991/issue30/3038.html*

4. *http://www.dictionary.com*

5. Elizabeth Janeway, "Women: Their Changing Roles," *The New York Times, The Great Contemporary Issues Series,* Set 1, Vol. 4 (New York, Arno Press, 1978), 7.

6. Scott Miller, *Rebels with Applause: Broadway's Ground-Breaking Musicals* (Portsmouth, NH: Heinemann Publishing, 2001).

7. *Strong's Concordance*

8. Ibid.

9. Ibid.

10. Ibid.

11. The Holy Bible: New International Version (NIV). Copyright © 1973, 1978, 1984 by Biblica.

12. *Strong's Concordance*

13. George W. Gilmore, *The New Schaff-Herzog Encyclopedia of Religious Knowledge* (Grand Rapids, MI: Baker House Books, 1954).

14. *www.avalon.law.yale.edu/imt/08-05-46.asp*

[15] Ruth Freeman Swain, *Hairdo! What We Do and Did to our Hair* (New York, NY: Holiday House, 2002).

[16] Gail Duff, *Natural Beauty: Making and Using Pure and Simple Beauty Products* (Hong Kong: Breslich & Foss, Ltd., 1998).

[17] Kevin Mancuso, *The Mane Thing* (New York, NY: Little, Brown and Company, 1999).